CONTENTS

FOREWORD

R I Mawby

Principal Lecturer in Social Policy

Department of Social & Political Studies

Plymouth Polytechnic

It is less than twenty years since material on the police was almost entirely dominated by material from the United States. In that short time, however, a wealth of research and expertise has emerged in Britain, combining theoretical strengths with practical foci, as is well illustrated in the papers included here.

All the speakers reflect on issues of particular relevance to the role, function, and operation of the police in British society in the late 1980s, and in particular address the key areas of accountability and community.

The police sometimes, I think, see themselves as "piggy in the middle" between their political masters who prescribe law and its implementation and the public. Alternatively they may be seen as protected by a fortress of professional autonomy from the influence of both the political machinery of government and the community they allegedly serve. There is, therefore, a firm link between politics and public, between political control and community ties.

This link is illustrated in many of the sessions. In the first Rod Morgan focusses on consultation and police accountability, both in political terms and in the practical outcomes of the police community consultation committees set up under the 1984 Police and Criminal Evidence Act. He argues that the legitimacy of such committees is problematic where community groups are not represented, and that where community views on appropriate police policies are so diverse and pluralistic both community accountability and local political accountability tend not to represent the perspectives of those most critical of the police.

Interestingly, Dave Wall's paper, on the office of Chief Constable, echoes some of these points. He argues, for example, that in the early days County Chief Constables were drawn from a land owning rural elite, whereas Borough Chief Constables were more representative - of both police and public. However, while in the former case the reason was to leave police policies in the hands of "one of their own", in the latter it reflected the wish of the Watch Committees in the Boroughs to have an employee. in charge who would carry out their orders. Against both these influences, Wall sees the current model as one of the autonomous professional, where the Chief Constable is *See Lecture* certainly more representative of the public - in terms of his background - but is insulated from that same public by his work experience and professional or managerial expertise.

Whilst these two contributions are very much focussed on the issues of power and control, the three remaining sessions have their roots in the community. Policing practices reflect a balance between the political agenda, the nature of the community being policed, and the occupational culture through which policies become translated in the process of being implemented. Gwyneth Kelland, in her contribution on the role of women in the police, stresses both the macho-image/danger/ excitement of police subculture and the wider sexist assumptions of our society in influencing the operation of equal employment philosophies within the police.

- 3 -

The last two papers incorporate the question of power and accountability in rather different ways by addressing policing in the context of public involvement in the processes of crime prevention and control. Trevor Bennett, who has been immersed in a study of neighbourhood watch schemes in different parts of London, looks at the origins of neighbourhood watch in the US and in the light of his study the likely development of schemes throughout Britain. Some neighbourhood watch schemes of course involve the special constabulary, which is, along with neighbourhood watch, exciting considerable government interest at present due to the possibility of addressing the "crime problem" with minimum additional resources. Martin Gill's research, which was based in the South West, involved victim support and probation volunteers as well as police specials. Here, however he concentrates on the police and, in particular, on the relationship between specials and regular officers. Interestingly, he argues that the motivations specific to applicants to the special constabulary, combined with their eagerness to become a valued part of the force, constrains any possibility of their being public watchdogs. Again then, public involvement in policing is no guarantee of a broader base for police/community relations.

These few brief points well illustrate the fact that while much current research is policy-oriented, cosy political solutions are less tangible. Overall, perhaps, this set of conference papers raises a number of issues concerning the place of the police in Britain today, which will act as a stimulus to both academics and practitioners.

CONSULTATION AND POLICE ACCOUNTABILITY[1]

R Morgan

Senior Lecturer,

University of Bath

Introduction

Bayley (1983, 146) defines an accountable police force as one 'whose
actions, severally and collectively, are congruent with the values of
the community in which it works and responsive to the discrepancies
when they are pointed out'. The conclusion he draws from a comparative
international review of policing is that there is no evidence to
support the contention that anyone device - constitutional, legal
administrative or managerial - is either a necessary or sufficient
condition for police accountability as he defines it. He recommends a
pragmatic approach: the devices that need to be adopted in any one
country depend on the historical legacy and the particular conjunction
of circumstances prevailing.

Bayley's definition has advantages and disadvantages. It is
attractive because of its panoramic diffuseness and because it focuses
on outcomes established empirically. It deliberately glides over the

- 5 -

distinction between the accountability of, as opposed to the control over, an agency. It encompasses all dimensions of accountability - political (external) and managerial (internal) - and covers all types of accounts - audit (propriety), procedural (efficiency) and programme (effectiveness) (Robinson, 1971; Stewart, 1984). It therefore enables the analyst to avoid the definitional stops set up by those legalistic and narrowly programmatic approaches to accountability which dominate discussions of policing in Britain. The disadvantage of Bayley's definition lies in its operationalisation. Its breadth, and the limitless inquiry required to establish it, may in the end mean that critical senses are blunted because judgements are endlessly deferred. Which of the many competing 'community values' are to be included? How, given the incommensurable demands made on the police, is policy 'congruence' to be assessed? And how is 'discrepancy' pointed out and 'responsiveness' to be defined? The research difficulties are so legion that one suspects Bayley's comparative conclusion is more a product of his elusive method than the comprehensiveness and rigour of his evidence.

Yet Bayley's end-state concept is a useful starting point for thinking about the police accountability debate in Britain. I assume that the protagonists in the current disputes regarding what powers the police should have, how complaints against the police should be investigated, or what changes should be made to the constitutional arrangements for police governance, accept Bayley's statement as the goal of accountability. I assume that all discussants have in good faith concluded that the particular circumstances now prevailing in Britain make each of their prescriptions necessary or sufficient conditions for Bayley's end-state to prevail. My purpose in this paper is to reach behind these political judgements and speculate how they are likely to be affected by a policy initiative currently being pursued by the Government, namely the introduction of police community consultation committees under s,106 of the Police and Criminal Evidence Act 1984 (PACEA).

Accountability and Consultation: The Background Argument

Since 'law and order' seems likely to be a prominent feature in the forthcoming general election, as it was in 1979, we had best begin our review with the positions the main political parties are adopting vis a vis accountability and consultation. The Labour Party argues that the Government, by its pursuit of public expenditure cuts and the creation of mass unemployment, has deepened the divisions in British society and, contrary to its law and order rhetoric, promoted a crime wave and failed to protect the public. By contrast the Government argues that the Labour Party has little regard for the rule of law and is at root anti-police. A substantial part of the evidence for the latter claim comprises Labour plans for reforming existing arrangements for the governance of the police. This argument, which until recently seemed to be of interest only to constitutional lawyers, now carries a good deal of party political symbolic baggage.

The positions so far taken up by the main political parties on the governance of the police can broadly be labelled retentionist, reformist and radical. The Government is firmly wedded to the arrangements embodied in the Police Act 1964 - that is the 'tripartite' partnership between police authorities, chief constables and the Home Secretary, and the doctrine of constabulary independence. Yet though committed to retaining this basic framework, the Government has, like previous administrations, adapted it to fit its analysis of current conditions: the configuration within the tripartite structure has changed substantially since 1964 and has not stood still since 1979. The Government's initiatives have been the product of both criticisms specific to the police - ranging from the suggestions of professional insensitivity high-lighted by the Scarman Report (1981) to doubts about service effectiveness expressed in research reports from the Home Office Research and Planning Unit (Clark and Hough, 1981; Heal et al, 1986) - and the application to the police of Government policy on public sector service generally (Prime Minister, 1984).

Two ostensibly countervailing tendencies are apparent. First, there has been yet more centralised control by the Home Office over the direction of police policy. The Metropolitan Authorities have been swept away and replaced by constitutionally and financially weakened Joint Boards (Loveday, 1985; Loveday, 1987). The Association of Chief Police Officers (ACPO) has grown in importance and been drawn further into corporate decision making. The Home Secretary has made increased use of his powers under s.28 in the name of service efficiency. And overall budgetary control has been tightened, backed up by increased use of Home Office circulars for policy formation and implementation (Weatheritt 1986). Yet, secondly, this firmer hand on the central tiller has been used to promote a measure of what is claimed to be decentralisation. Despite the wording of s.106 and the orthodox obeisance to local autonomy and flexibility expressed in ministerial speeches and Home Office Circulars (54/1982; 2/1985), in fact the Government has used every available device to impose a national blue print for local consultation arrangements (Morgan, 1986). Devolved managerial setting of objectives has been introduced in the Metropolitan police and encouraged in the provinces by a Home Office Circular (114/1983) and H.M. Inspectorate of Constabulary. Further, the same Circular makes clear that agreement between chief constables and police authorities is a pre-condition of Home Office approval for further resources. Finally, the Government has commended the setting up of local lay visitor to police station schemes (HO 12/1986). Yet though the decentralising initiatives involve police authorities (the boroughs in London) they do not provide for increased local political accountability: no sanctions have made available to authorities in the event of their disagreeing with chief constables over policy. Though there is a proper distinction between accountability to an elected body for policy (ex post facto explanations for use of delegated powers) as opposed to control of policy by an elected body (ex ante direction), no definition of political accountability has meaning in the absence of formal sanctions which can be applied to those who exercise delegated powers contrary to the wishes of an elected body. In fact the Government's initiatives are based, as were the recommendations in Lord Scarman's Report, rather on a concept of professional accountability (see Kogan, 1986). The police retain policy making independence but are now: to be better trained; to make management and routine decisions more transparently; and to sensitise themselves to community opinion through the various initiatives described above. By these means, so the argument goes, the police will forge a partnership with the community (Home Office, 1986), will continuously renew their mandate to 'police by consent', and will ensure, to return to Bayley's definition, that their priorities and methods are congruent with those approved of by the community.

The Alliance has adopted a reformist position on these questions. It condemns equally those 'extremist Labour councillors (who) seek out every possible opportunity to undermine the police and try to introduce local political control over police operations' and the 'Government's increasingly centralist tendency' (Owen and Steel 1987, 84-5). It supports the Government's initiatives to increase police sensitivity to consumer opinion, but proposes that the notion of partnership - between central and local government, and between police officers, politicians and community leaders locally - be given firmer roots and greater clarity within the tripartite structure. The contours of Alliance policy are not wholly clear because it proposes appointing a new Royal Commission to consider the arrangements for the governance of the police. However, sympathies lie with reform of police authority membership: it would like to reduce the proportion of elected members and replace them with 'other community representatives ... to be appointed by the Home Secretary' (SDP 1985,22), and recommend that the Government issue precise guidance on the relative powers and responsibilities of the parties to the tripartite structure so as to encourage police authorities to exercise their existing duties more vigorously. The latter proposal has a well established lineage (Scarman, 1981; Regan, 1983).

The Labour Party advocates radical change to both the membership and powers of police authorities. Greater political accountability is for the Labour Party a precondition of a more co-operative relationship between police and public. Indeed contra the Government, the Labour Party analysis implicitly lays the blame for the diminished trust between police and certain sections of the community - notably the young and ethnic minorities - on excessive reliance on professional autonomy. The Labour Party (1981. para 5.3) shares Lord Scarman's view that the police are in danger of becoming 'a corps d'elite' set apart from the rest of the community', but by definition rejects Lord Scarman's reliance on enhanced professionalisation. It argues that the police ' like any other public service' must allow 'members of the local community ... through their elected representatives ... to have a say in how policing is run'. Chief constables should not 'alone decide policing policies and priorities'. Accordingly 'the next Labour Government will remove non-elected magistrates (currently one third of the membership) from police committees'. Police authorities will, subject to 'minimum standards set down by Parliament' and a statutory duty 'to enforce the law', be given powers to 'decide the nature of policing in their area.' This will mean that the 'chief constable's relationship with the authority would be similar to that of any other local council chief officer' (Labour Party, 1986).

It follows logically that the stance taken by the three political parties on local police community consultation differs fundamentally. Though all are agreed that consultation is a good thing, for Conservatives it is the pivotal mechanism for ensuring retention of police professional independence and insulating the police form political control locally. If consultation arrangements are seen everywhere to be in place, if it can be claimed that committees are working well and practical co-operation between police and public established, there is no case for tampering with the Police Act 1964. Accountability in Bayley's panoramic sense will have been secured without it. This explains why the Government, contrary to its defence of the very diffuse terms of s.106 (committees are not a statutory requirement in the provinces), has throughout the country pressurised chief constables and police authorities, many of whom were distinctly unenthusiastic, into setting up committees.

For the Alliance consultation is an adjunct, a safeguard, for the existing tripartite arrangement wishes to preserve but reform. Consultation, and the recruitment of non-elected community representatives to police authorities, is a means of better representing public opinion, a goal that will in the final analysis be more fully realised through proportional representation at all levels of government.

For the Labour Party, the Government's emphasis on consultation poses a dilemma. To support or not to support? To be involved or not? There are no readily acceptable reasons for opposing consultation per se. But the implications of flourishing consultation arrangements are readily apparent for the Labour programme. It is Catch 22. Not to participate is to risk the Party being labelled anti-police. To participate is to risk losing the case for radical reform. The Party has therefore commended consultation as an idea but has constantly reiterated that 'police consultation with the community is no substitute for accountability (Labour Party, 1986), by which is meant power to determine policy by locally elected police authorities.

The struggle between the political parties over consultation to capture territory for their different versions of police accountability has been waged most fiercely in London because of the unique constitutional position in the capital. In London the Home Secretary, as Police Authority for the Metropolitan Police, has used his specific powers under s.106 (3) to make consultative committees a statutory requirement. Further, as a symbolic gesture to local government, committees have been instituted by borough rather than, as is generally the case in the provinces police sub-divisions or divisions. On the Labour side, many inner-London boroughs initially boycotted the consultation initiatives, though, for reasons we have reviewed, the argument within the Party has since been largely resolved in favour of participation. However, the most recent illustration of the difficult position for the Labour Party on this issue is provided in a Briefing Paper on Police Accountability from the London Strategic Policy Unit (1987), the vestigial successor to the GLC Police Committee. The LSPU fully endorses the GLC proposals for a locally elected police authority for London but, in order to be 'realistic', proposes that change be introduced in two stages. The new authority should first take over the powers and functions currently exercised by the Home Secretary. The second stage, amending 'the present constitutional status of police constables' and 'the wider powers and responsibilities of police authorities' could come later.

Given that the Home Secretary exercises more power under the Metropolitan Police Act 1829 in relation to the Metropolitan Commissioner than do police authorities in the provinces under the Police Act 1964, this recommendation is more ingenious than ingenuous. It will be argued by the police and Government that the existing powers of the Home Secretary as Police Authority for London are justified by the national functions of the Metropolitan Police, functions which the LSPU propose be hived off to a national police agency and authority. It is inconceivable that any Government would grant to a locally elected police authority for London powers not enjoyed by authorities in the provinces. What the LSPU document in fact betrays are the misgivings entertained within the Labour Party, particularly among councillors (Morgan and Swift, 1987), that the Party's policies for radical changes to the arrangements for the governance of the police will be misunderstood by, or misrepresented to, the public: that they will be a hostage to electoral fortune.

The party political debate is mirrored among other, including academic, commentators. Police officers tend to argue that though they are primarily accountable to the law itself, nevertheless consultation will assist them better to work with the grain of community opinion. On the left, by contrast, there is no shortage of those who argue with Spencer that the Government's consultative arrangements suggest powers that are illusory and are nothing short of 'an attempt to appease increasing demands for accountability by offering a palliative which neither increases community control nor weakens police autonomy'. (Spencer, 1985, 106; see also Christian, 1983; GLC, 1985; Scraton, 1985).

Not all academic commentators are so damning however. For example, though Kinsey, Lea and Young argue unequivocally for empowering police authorities to determine policy, they do not suggest that constitutional changes will solve all the ills in police community relations and policing methods they diagnose. Consultation, they argue, will be necessary whatever the constitutional framework. It will assist the police authority in formulating its general strategy and the police in identifying particular problems: community groups could discuss crime prevention strategies with officers; women's groups discuss methods for combatting sexual harassment; and ethnic minorities review with the police techniques for combatting racial attacks (Kinsey et al, 1986, 180). And though they argue that within the new constitutional framework consultational groups would be very different from the current community liaison panels, they cite no reasons why benefits to policy and relationships could not accrue under existing conditions. They assume that the current initiatives are cosmetic, symbolic. rather than substantive, a 'bureaucratic police-public relations exercise' (ibid,181). But in fact their approach to consultation suggests a different set of possibilities, namely, that whatever framework for political accountability exists there is need for continuous grass-roots discourse between consumers and professionals and the development of an ethos of professional sensitivity to the rights and interests of vulnerable minorities. The fact that the Government may have introduced, inter alia, consultation as a means to counter radical constitutional change, does not rule out the possibility of a shift in the influences that are brought to bear on policy. Symbolic intentions may have substantive outcomes.

For the question neglected by much of the party political debate on police accountability concerns the relationship between political and managerial accountability. If accountability refers to the liability of one who exercises delegated responsibility to render an explanation for actions taken, and in the final analysis the liability of that person to sanctions in the event of the explanation being judged unsatisfactory, then clearly no one can be held accountable to another without his being accountable for something. In the case of policing this poses two problems: first, the contingent, heterogeneous, ambiguous, inherently contradictory and contentious nature of the police mandate; second, the relative invisibility of police actions (see Bradley et al, 1986 for full discussion). There are plenty of politicians who will agree with an experienced and influential Labour county councillor member of a police authority we interviewed during our research who doubted that the Labour Party policies would, if implemented, make a great deal of difference to the degree of control actually exercised by police authorities:

> What would a general operational statement look like? Would it be any more precise than the generalities of policing objectives which the police are now stating? What would prevent those general statements substantially being ignored in practice, either because it was said that day-to-day exigencies required it, or because senior personnel could not effectively control what junior personnel were doing? In the event of disagreement it would be the Home Secretary who would determine the actual direction of policy, as he does already.

This councillor took the practical view that the way forward lay in using consultative committees to get middle management officers used to the unfamilar idea of talking regularly and frankly to local politicians without fear of "losing their operational virginity", an aspiration remarkably similar to Kinsey, Lea dn Young's (1986, 181) wish to establish a venue within which "rank and file officers could... speak freely about the strains and problems" of their work. However, whereas the latter commentators assume this cannot be achieved without constitutional change, this councillor saw no reason why the process could not just as well take place under current conditions. Some analysts of policy appear to agree with him. For example, Reiner, (1985, 180-1), though accepting that there "are no valid constitutional or historical grounds in principle for exempting the police from democratically-elected policy-making authorities" doubts they are either "necessary or sufficient for accomplishing the goal of a police force whose operations are 'democratic'". Externally imposed institutions may be resented by the police and lead to a closing of ranks, thereby reducing rather than increasing police sensitivity to public opinion. On these grounds consultative committees, without formal powers, may prove more effective mechanisms for influencing policy (see also Savage, 1984).

Consultative Committees: Aspirations and Operation

In the space available it is possible to give no more than a crude pen picture of the form of consultation committees and the hopes the Government entertain for them. There is a good deal of variation from one part of the country to another. Nevertheless, from the Home Office Circulars (54/1982 and 2/1985) and ministerial statements, the official purposes of consultation committees can be summarised as follows.

Consumer Demand. What is to count as the measure of police effectiveness must constantly be appraised in the light of what concerns the public and what the community considers policing priorities ought to be. Formal consultation, it is suggested, provides a mechanism through which the public will be able to articulate their consumer needs and wants. And it should reduce the danger of the police, by virtue of their increasing specialisation and reliance on technology, becoming out of touch with public opinion and framing operational policies divorced from public opinion.

Consumer Education. If the police are to be more responsive to consumer demand, then the corollary is that the public must be educated as to police limitations. They must understand the problems the police confront and appreciate that legal and resource restrictions mean priorities have to be chosen. The public must be discouraged from developing unrealistic expectations. Further, the many and varied demands made on the police often conflict or are incommensurable: the trade-offs between police services, a complex question which the police have themselves only recently begun systematically to address, will have to be explained to the public.

Legitimacy/Public Relations. The claim that policing is by consent can only ever be true in a broad sense. Policing will always involve the use of coercive powers, and in the final resort force, against individuals and groups. Nevertheless the doctrine of policing by consent must be sustained by evidence that the police listen to groups in conflict with them. Consultation provides a means for building bridges, for the police to explain their obligations and for groups critical of them to explain their perceptions, interests and frustrations.

Crime Prevention. If the police are dependant on assistance and information from the public to be effective and efficient then crime prevention is a joint process and the community must learn to shoulder its responsibilities regarding it. Local consultation groups can be the springboard for mobilising community support for the police. When the public have learnt to trust the police and have begun to appreciate better their problems and limitations, then will be the time to initiate communitarian crime prevention strategies like neighbourhood watch. Consultative groups can stimulate the policy equivalent in the policing field of the self-help (privatisation and voluntarisation) approach the Government has adopted with regard to public sector services generally. If successful, these schemes can assist control of public expenditure on policing.

Though implementation of the consultation policy varies, the following generalisations cover the arrangements typical of most areas (for full details by police authority see Morgan and Maggs, 1985):

(i)   all but one or two of the 43 police authorities in England and Wales have set up formal police community consultative committees with force-wide constitutions and terms of reference closely modelled on Home Office Circulars 54/1982 and 2/1985.

(ii)   consultative committees are in most cases based on police sub-divisions rather than local authority areas: this emphasises police local administration rather than the political accountability of local government. This is not true, as I have indicated above, in London, where committees are based on boroughs. However, in London the committees are quite explicitly police-initiated and not under the control of borough councils (Commissioner, 1985a and 1985b).

(iii)   committees generally meet quarterly, are chaired by elected members of the police authority (though not in London where there is no locally elected police authority), and typically have 15-25 members appointed partly or wholly by the police authority. In a few areas what we may term the 'forum' model has been adopted. Here committees are larger (typically any community organisation with a written constitution and a given number of members can send a representative) and tend to meet more frequently. They tend also to elect their own chairpersons.

(iv)   committees usually meet in local authority or neighbourhood premises rather than police stations, and invariably make provision for parts of meetings, or occasional meetings, to be open to the public. The publicity for meetings is generally poor though in a few areas this is conspicuously not the case.

(v)   the membership of committees typically includes representatives of: county district and parish councils; the principal statutory services (invariably education and youth services, sometimes social services, housing, leisure, probation etc); the churches; trades councils and/or chambers of commerce; ethnic minority organisations; residents' and tenants' associations; neighbourhood action groups; and voluntary service organisations, particularly those for the aged and young. The police, if not actually members, are most usually represented by the sub-divisional superintendent, and attend as of right.

(vi)   committee members are seldom under 30 years of age and are typically active 'respectable' members of the community. They represent one organisation (in the simple sense that they are members of it) and are usually involved in others. Generally speaking they are <u>not</u> the sort of people who have previously had much contact with the police (except possibly socially) and, though they know little of the police, are invariably well-disposed towards them. They are generally not people who have been in conflict with the police or have adverse personal experience of them.

(vii)   few forces provide committees with any back-up staff and finance. Where support is provided it is usually only to assist with arrangements for fixing venues, taking minutes, sending out invitations etc. Most committees are provided with no more than a small annual budget to cover the hire of halls, postage etc. Consultative committees, like their parent police authorities, generally have no independent expert/research support.

(viii) most committee meetings are sustained by police effort. The police generally have to fill the agenda for want of lay members' contributions. The centrepieces of the majority of meetings are the sub-divisional commander's report (oral and/or in writing) and the 'guest presentation', most popularly a brief talk by a specialist police officer (crime prevention, drugs, schools liaison etc), though other non-police guest speakers appear occasionally.

Consequences

No brief generalised account can do justice to the variety of consultation practices which exist around the country. Variations are attributable to the commitment of particular police authorities or chief constables, and the dynamism of each committee is heavily dependent on the enthusiasm and will of chairpersons and local police commanders. Further, it cannot be said too often that these are early days. As I have hinted above, consultation involves police officers and lay members embarking on an essentially unknown terrain: it will take time for participants to find their feet, gather experience and decide what it is that they want to make of the opportunities opening out to them. And yet, certain initial patterns are sufficiently widespread to make them worthy of comment. We can begin to think about specific hypothesised consequences.

The competing hypotheses relating to the party political argument over future arrangements for the governance of the police can be stated as follows;-

The existence of PLC's will increase the legitimacy of the existing tripartite arrangements. It will do so because:

(a)   PLC's will involve the police, police authority members and a variety of community representatives

(b)   police officers will learn better about the manner in which police actions are viewed locally and will adjust policy to meet local needs and viewpoints

(c)   the police will furnish PLC's with fuller accounts of their operations

(d)   police authority members will learn more about policing (will be better educated about or become co-opted to police viewpoints) and will·develop more personal relationships with officers in management ranks

(e)   because better informed, police authority members will take their duties more seriously as a result of which the police will more fully consult them as part of their policy planning cycle (this course is recommended by Butler 1984)

(f)   police and police authority members will develop mutually trusting relationships and the demand for constitutional change will be diminished.

If any or all of these propositions fail in practice, it is possible to argue that the operation of consultative groups may produce the reverse consequences, namely increase the demand for radical reform. For example:

(a)   if significant political or community groups are unwilling to become involved in consultation and

(b)   the police do not adjust their policies in relation to those groups

(c)   or if the police either do not furnish the accounts which particular groups wish to receive, or the accounts do not reach the groups concerned

(d)   then contact between the police, politicians and community representatives may confirm the view that the police are under insufficient control and fuel the demand for constitutional change.

The early evidence suggests that in different places both these sequences have been set in train. However, our overall impression is that in most places consultation committees are serving to legitimate police policy and will probably undermine support for radical constitutional change.

First, political party and police service participation is almost comprehensively the norm. Whereas many police authority councillors and sub-divisional commanders embarked on formal consultation sceptically - many of them claiming the exercise would prove a temporary phenomenon doomed to whither on the vine - consultation committees have become a fixed feature on the landscape. There is considerable pressure from the centre (nationally from the Home Office and locally from Force HQ's) to ensure that committees are seen to operate. Sub-divisional commanders now regard their links with committees as part of their management task. Indeed in many forces sub-divisional commanders are told unequivocally that they will be judged by their success with committees (see Commissioner 1985b). No matter how much individuals consider committees a waste of time - and many councillors and middle ranking police officers take that view - few are prepared to say so publicly: they see it as their duty to make positive efforts to nurture the work of the committees to which they are attached. It is now rare for committees to be boycotted by local politicians.

Second, most committees are not used, as many police officers feared, as platforms for criticism of the police. On the contrary, those groups most critical of the police (the young and the ethnic minorities) are generally conspicuous by their absence: consultative committees tend to be deferential to police judgements and supportive of them. Members, including police authority members, become better informed about policing matters as a consequence of their participation. They also become more sympathetic to police problems and police solutions to those problems. Members of all party political persuasions tend to agree that the demands made on the police are outstripping their resources and that resources should be given to the police.

Third, the police are undoubtedly providing more information about resource distribution and routine decision making than used to be the case. Subdivisional commanders tend increasingly to furnish their committees with details of local staff, their beats, specialisations and shift systems, local patterns of recorded crime, and, when major events and operations occur, details of police operations. This increased openness about policy cannot be attributed to the emergence of consultative groups alone: it is as much the product of changes in police styles of management which have in turn been influenced, inter alia, by the Government's Financial Management Initiative. Most councillors express support for the policies and management styles of their local police forces and there is little evidence of local politicians asking for information which the police deny them. Indeed, there is evidence that in those forces where chief constables have invited local politicians to assist in the policy formation process - determining priorities and setting objectives etc - they have evoked little response.

Against these pictures of co-operation and satisfaction we have to set some vital pieces of contrary evidence. First, those groups least happy with the police are least involved in consultation. Insofar as consultative groups are functioning as receptors of consumer opinion, they are largely failing with respect to those consumers whose experience of police actions is most adverse. For example, the Afro-Caribbean community has in many areas decided that consultative groups are not worth their time and effort: it is widely believed committees are creatures of the police and that nothing they do will change police policy. They have no power. It follows that committees seldom serve directly as bridge-building venues.

The fact that consultative committees generally fail to incorporate groups critical of the police is not necessarily evidence against the constitutional legitimation hypothesis however. The sections of the community marginal to police community consultation tend also to be marginal to party politics. For example, most councillors report that whereas constituents regularly bring to them casework concerning such services as planning, housing, education etc, they are rarely asked to take up policing matters. And without such prompting few councillors ask penetrating questions about day to day police policy.

Only where a police operation is large, costly and visible, or triggers a major disturbance, do the views of marginal groups generally impinge on police authority politics. They do so in part because major police operations generally reveal for all to see how, in the final analysis, the police decide what the problems are and how they should be solved. Though the police may justify major operational decisions on the basis of concerns expressed to them by members of the public through telephone calls, correspondence and consultation formal and informal, senior officers seldom consider it wise to spell out in advance the operational options for dealing with these concerns or take politicians into their confidence about decisions they are actively considering. If councillors are informed in advance about a major operation, it is usually only a matter of hours before it is put into effect: by then the police are already moving against the mass trespass, flying pickets, ghetto drug dealers, or whatever group is concerned. What the police hope is that those councillors informed will stand up and support the operational decisions taken. However, even when this is the outcome, it is apparent there has not been consultation about the operation per se. Not infrequently this results in politicians or community leaders being disowned as impotent puppets by their political colleagues or the community groups they allegedly represent. This sequence was well illustrated in the case of 'Operation Delivery' in Bristol in September 1986: the immediate result was that the position of the chairpersons of the two consultative committees in St Paul's became untenable and the Labour chair of the Police Authority felt obliged to resign his seat.

This type of incident undoubtedly provokes considerable discord and renews the aspiration, for at least some councillors, to empower police authorities to determine policy. Significantly, the most sophisticated analysis so far produced of what this would mean practically, accepts the police view that no clear distinction can be drawn between 'general policy' and 'operational decisions' (Lustgarten 1986; see also Spencer 1985). On the grounds that the term 'operational' is obfuscatory, and that most so-called operational decisions are essentially political, Lustgarten (1986, 172) argues that though the 'investigation or surveillance of specific persons or specific crimes should remain entirely under the direction of the police', all other policy issues, including 'search operations in particular areas' should be subject to police authority direction. By contrast the police maintain that the fact that no easy dividing line can be drawn between general and day-to-day policy is the most important argument for leaving policy-making where it is, with the professionals.

The question begged by Lustgarten's approach is, at what point does a police action against 'specific persons or specific crimes' become a 'search operation of the area'? Even were county councillors to have the detailed policy-making powers that Lustgarten proposes (and our evidence suggests that most Labour members do not wish it), and the police were obliged to lay before them for approval plans to undertake the sort of large-scale operations witnessed in Lambeth, Handsworth and Bristol in recent months, the police would inevitably begin to back up their operational proposals with evidence of consumer demands. Computerised logging of messages to the police now makes this sort of assessment relatively simple.

To some extent this is what is already happening alongside consultative committees as currently constituted, and it is limited evidence for the argument that committees may enhance accountability in the broad sense of the term. It is a commonplace in the literature on formal consultation procedures in other public sector services that inasmuch as committee members are appointed or self-appointed they may either be unrepresentative or fail actively to represent (Richardson, 1983; Boaden et al, 1982). Members may, as I have implicitly suggested above, easily be co-opted to the professionals' standpoint. Consultation may (as may local elections) fail to produce persons who express the viewpoints or defend the interests of economically or politically marginal groups. In which case minority rights may be no better protected. Indeed marginal groups may further be marginalised: some Labour councillors argue against control of policy by police authorities on precisely these grounds. Yet insofar as the police, following the introduction of consultative committees, find it necessary to justify their policies by reference to consumer opinion, the political status of those policy decisions is undeniably altered. The police can either appeal to the support of consultative committee members, or, if they consider their opinions unrepresentative, the requests of other groups asking for police action.

In either case, the existence of consultative groups has knock-on consequences for policy formation. Councillors, community leaders or group spokespersons may or may or not be representative, but no longer is it plausible for critics of police policy to claim that the police are acting straightforwardly against the community. The debate is now firmly within the community where, whatever the rights and wrongs of specific police operations, there are clearly an abundance of competing interests and views about police policy. And herein lies the deficiency of consultative committees as presently constituted. Consultative committees may contribute to the opening up of police policy. They may, under certain circumstances, lead the police to seek out or record opinions not represented within local committees. But in the event of their being competing or incommensurable demands for police services, as seems probable under most circumstances, the final undeniably political decisions about priorities and solutions, remain with the police.

Conclusions

Most parts of the country have not experienced at first hand large-scale controversial police operations which expose deep divisions about priorities or methods. Adverse experience of the police generally occurs within individual private encounters which seldom result in official complaints or representations to politicians. As a consequence those persons who make up consultative committees, generally the local great and the good, including politicians, have little basis for challenging the police accounts they receive and seldom do so. They tend to have positive attitudes towards the police when they join committees, are impressed with what they hear from officers and become more sympathetic to them as a result of participation. Most Conservative and Alliance councillors see no reason to tamper with the independence which the police currently enjoy, and though a majority of Labour members think that as a matter of principle there is a case for greater political accountability, in practice they are impressed by the professional standards of officers and have no great wish themselves to become responsible for operational decisions. As the police become more open about their priorities and objectives, about the basis on which they make their policy decisions, and about the consequences of their distribution of resources, so increasingly do politicians doubt whether empowering police authorities to make policy would make much difference to the direction of policy. There is reason to believe that the operation of consultation committees is serving to bolster the present arrangements for the governance of the police.

Major police operations leading to disturbances and controversy expose the fact that politicians involved in consultation are not responsible for the policy decisions which, on occasion, they are invited to support. Such policy decisions have irrefutably a political as well as a legal dimension: they require judgements to be made on the relative merits of competing cases for policing priorities and the use of different operational options. If the consequence of police decisions involves alleged discrimination against a section of the community, then politicians involved in consultation are increasingly unable to shelter behind the skirts of professional neutrality. They also must make public pronouncements as to whether they consider the professionals have judged correctly. In circumstances where the police fail adequately to justify their decisions by reference to consumers' wishes, the demand by local politicians that they rather than the police should have control of policy is kept vigorously alive. However, the evidence suggests that the police are learning to provide such evidence.

The operation of consultative groups may not greatly assist the most disadvantaged sections of the community. However, for as long as those groups are marginal to the party political process there is no very convincing case for arguing that their interests would be better protected were police authorities empowered to frame policy. In the provinces consultative committees are already a police authority not a police responsibility. There are few grounds for believing that marginal groups would be any more prepared to participate in committee deliberations were the powers of police authority - which in any case few members of the public understand - to be increased.

There is one hypothesis to set against this conclusion. Police authority politics are in many respects the politics of irresponsibility, the consequence of the party political divide over law and order issues. Many Conservative councillors almost steadfastly do not call the police to account on the grounds that to do so would suggest a lack of confidence. Many Labour councillors adopt a belligerently posturing stance vis a vis the police conspicuously to demonstrate their radical virility. On both sides there is little effort to get to grips with the detail of policy and to assist the police with the very real dilemmas confronting them. It could be argued that on both sides of the political spectrum, councillors would act more responsibly, would be prepared to invest more effort in their duties, including consultation, were they constitutionally responsible for policy.

Footnotes

1.   The data on which this paper is based were collected as part of an ongoing research project on police community consultation processes funded by the Economic and Social Research Council and the Police Foundation. I am indebted to my colleague Mr. Paul Swift for his assistance in that research. Responsibility for the contents of this paper is, however, entirely my own.

References

Bayley D.H. (1983) 'Accountability and Control of the Police: Some Lessons for Britain' in Bennett, T. (ed) The Future of Policing, Cambridge: Cropwood Conference Series No 15.

Boaden N., Goldsmith M., Hampton W. and Stringer P. (1982) Public Participation in Local Services, London: Longmans.

Bradley D., Walker N. and Wilkie R. (1986) Managing the Police: Law Organisation and Democracy, London: Harvester.

Butler A.J.P. (1984) 'Policing by Objectives'. Paper presented to the British Association, Norwich, September.

Charke R.V.G. and Hough J.M. (eds) (1980) The Effectiveness of Policing, Farnborough: Gower.

Christian L. (1983) Policing by Coercion, London: GLC Police Support Unit.

Commissioner of the Metropolitan Police

    (1985a)   Instruction - Consultative Procedures, s.106 PACE, A7 Branch, February.

    (1985b)   Instruction - the Role of Police Officers in the Consultative Group, February.

Greater London Council (1983) A New Police Authority for London, Police Committee Discussion Paper No. 1, London: GLC.

Heal K., Tarling R. and Burrows J. (eds) (1985) Policing Today, London: HMSO.

Home Office (1986) Criminal Justice: a Working Paper, 2nd edition, London: Home Office.

Home Office Circulars:

    54/1982   Local Consultation Arrangements between the Community and the Police

    114/1983   Manpower, Effectiveness and Efficiency in the Police Service

    8/1984   Crime Prevention

    2/1985   Arrangements for Local Consultation between the Community and the Police Outside London

    12/1986   Lay Visitors to Police Stations

Kinsey R., Lea J. and Young J. (1986) Losing the Fight Against
    Crime, Oxford: Blackwell.

Kogan M. (1986) Education Accountability: an Analytic Overview,
    London: Hutchinson.

Labour Party (1986) Protecting Our People, London: Labour Party.

London Strategic Policy Unit (1987) Police Accountability: and a new
    strategic authority for London, London: LSPU.

Loveday B. (1985) 'The proposed Metropolitan Joint Boards for police,
    a critical evaluation', Policing, Winter.

Loveday B. (1987) Joint Boards for the Police: the impact of
    structural change on police governance in the Metropolitan
    Areas, Occasional Paper, City of Birmingham Polytechnic.

Lustgarten L. (1986) The Governance of the Police, London: Sweet and
    Maxwell.

Morgan R. and Maggs C. (1985) Setting the P.A.C.E.: Police Community
    Consultation Arrangements in England and Wales, Centre for the
    Analysis of Social Policy, University of Bath.

Morgan R. (1986) 'Police Consultative Groups: the Implications for the
    Governance of the Police', Political Quarterly, January-March.

Morgan R. (1987) 'The Police' in Harrison A., Gretton J. and
    Parkinson M. (eds) Reshaping Local Government, London: Policy
    Journals (forthcoming).

Morgan R. and Swift P. (1987) 'The Future of Police Authorities:
    Members' Views' (forthcoming).

Owen D. and Steel D. (1987) The Time Has Come: Partnership for
    Progress, London: Weidenfeld.

Prime Minister (1984) Progress in Financial Management in Government
    Departments, (Cmnd 9297), London: HMSO.

Regan D. (1983) Are The Police Under Control, London: Social Affairs
    Unit.

Reiner R. (1985) The Politics of the Police, London: Wheatsheaf.

Richardson A. (1983) Participation, London: Routledge.

Robinson D. (1971) 'Government Contracting for Academic Research:
    Accountability in the American Experience' in Bruce L., Smith
    and Hague D. (eds) The Dilemma of Accountability in Modern
    Government, London: Macmillan.

Savage S. (1984) 'Political Control or Community Liaison?' Political
    Quarterly, Vol 55, January-March.

Lord Scarman (1981) Report of an Inquiry into the Brixton Disorder,
    10-12th April 1981, HMSO.

Scraton P. (1985) The State of the Police, London: Pluto.

SDP (1985) Crime and Policing, London: Social Democratic Party.

Spencer S. (1985) Called to Account: the Case for Police
    Accountability in England and Wales, London: NCCL.

Stewart J. (1984) 'The Role of Information in Public Accountability'
    in Hopwood A. and Tomkins C. (eds) Issues in Public Sector
    Accounting, London: Philip Allen.

Weatheritt M. (1986) Innovations in Policing, London: Croom Helm.

Widdicombe Report (1986) The Conduct of Local Authority Business:
    Report of the Committee of Inquiry into the Conduct of Local
    Authority Business, London: HMSO.

NEIGHBOURHOOD WATCH: PRINCIPLES AND PRACTICES

T Bennett

Senior Research Associate

Institute of Criminology

University of Cambridge

Introduction

Neighbourhood Watch (NW) is a relatively new addition to the list of measures used around the world to prevent crime. The implementation of NW schemes in Britain has received a mixed reception: on the one hand there are those who see it as almost a panacea capable of rebuilding communities, forging new and productive relationships between the public and the police and reducing crime; on the other hand there are those who see it as divisive, diverting police resources from poorer to richer communities and ineffective in achieving its aims. This paper examines the principles underlying NW and the way in which these principles are converted into practice. In particular, it aims to draw out some of the issues most frequently raised in discussions relating to NW and to introduce a few other issues less frequently discussed.

Background: the theoretical context of NW

The background of NW lies in part in early North American community-based crime prevention programmes. The growth of community crime prevention in the United States over the last half century has been guided by two major perspectives on the relationship between the community and crime: the first is the 'social disorganisation' or 'social control' perspective; and the second is the 'situational' or 'victimisation' perspective.

The 'Social Disorganisation' Perspective

The earliest version of the social disorganisation perspective can be found in the works of the Chicago sociologists of the 1920s and 1930s. The main argument in their writings is that as traditional communities become urbanised and industrialised they become socially disorganised and crime-prone. Social disorganisation leads to crime in part through an erosion of community norms and in part through an erosion of the community's ability to enforce rules. The erosion of community norms means that standards set by the community become weakened and delinquency and other forms of deviancy become tolerated and even accepted as a part of community life. The erosion of the community's ability to enforce rules means that community members no longer feel responsible for social control in their area and relegate their responsibility to formal organisations like the church, the school, the police and the courts who take over as rule enforcers.

As the early Chicago sociologists saw social disorganisation as the cause of increasing crime in communities, it is not surprising that they saw social organisation as the appropriate means of reducing crime. In 1932, the Chicago Area Project was established which was one of the first and one of the largest community crime prevention programmes in North America. The programme was unique in that it was created out of academic theory and empirical research. The major aim of the project was to integrate and organise communities. This was done by bringing together local residents and local institutions (churches, unions, business groups, sports clubs etc) to work together in creating community programmes. It was not considered important what kinds of programmes were developed and it was not considered necessary that the programmes directly concerned delinquents or delinquency prevention. The important thing was that they all, in some way, operated for the benefit of the community as a whole. Their underlying aim was to generate a spirit of self-help and self-determination and this was done by carrying out activities which fostered active control over the community. Such activities included the planning and operation of summer camps and community centres, health and sanitation programmes, improvements in schools, development of parent-teacher associations and campaigns for general environmental improvements.

> It is suggested that one way in which current methods of dealing with the problem of delinquency in high-rate areas may be strengthened is through programs of community action, initiated and carried on by the concerted efforts of citizens and local residents interested in improvements of community life in all its aspects. Such programs provide an opportunity to all residents to use their talents, energies, interests, and understanding in a common effort to strengthen, unify, and extend the constructive forces of the community.
> (Shaw and McKay, 1969, 322)

By the 1950s, the social disorganisation perspective fell into disfavour, but its core assumptions, concerning the importance of local community organisations as a means of re-establishing social control, continued in other kinds of community crime prevention programmes.

The Situational Perspective

Traditionally, situational prevention has focussed narrowly on efforts by individuals to secure their property or to protect themselves. Throughout the 1960s and 1970s these methods were extended, mainly in the United States of America, to include altering environments and communities. Instead of social organisation and social control as the focus, attention was shifted to the role of the community in the creation and prevention of opportunities for crime.

An implicit assumption underlying positivist criminological theory is that criminal behaviour is caused by inherited or acquired characteristics which predispose a person to crime. This emphasis on predispositional factors is sometimes referred to as a 'dispositional bias' (Clarke, 1980). Situational prevention does not share this bias. Instead it is based on the view that the motivation to offend is to some extent determined by situational factors. Offenders are not seen as compelled to crime as a result of misfortunes operating in their past histories, but as individuals who actively chose to offend in response to the constraints and inducements of particular situations. Situational crime prevention is based on this situational view of criminal behaviour. It is presumed that crimes can be prevented by altering the cost and reward balance of offending by increasing the constraints and reducing the inducements to crime. An important aspect of the development of this approach during the 1960s was that it was broadened to apply to whole communities. Methods were sought to devise programmes which would have an impact on the opportunity structure within entire neighbourhoods. An important contribution that communities could make in the prevention of crime, beyond what was possible for individuals alone, was their ability to provide comprehensive surveillance over a large area.

One of the best known community programmes based on the situational approach is the Hartford Crime Prevention Programme. The programme comprised three major elements affecting community organisation, policing and environmental design. The key assumptions underlying the programme were outlined in the evaluation report to the project. It was believed that crime in residential neighbourhoods was the product of the structure of opportunities for crime provided by the area and in order to reduce crime it was necessary to devise means of reducing these opportunities.

NW and the Two Perspectives
The main difference between the social disorganisation and situational perspectives is that in the former communities contribute to the creation of crime by losing their ability to define and enforce rules;

in the latter communities contribute to crime by creating or failing to block opportunities. The social disorganisation approach utilises methods which enhance informal social control; the situational prevention approach utilises methods which block opportunities.

It seems clear that in its simple form NW fits more comfortably within the framework of the situational approach. Its prime directives concern opportunity reduction in the form of encouraging neighbours to watch out and report suspicious activities to the police and to watch out for each others' homes when they are unoccupied. In this simple form, it is clear the NW is not about creating informal social control or integrating communities in the way defined by the social disorganisation perspective. The distinction between the two approaches is important because it affects the way in which NW is viewed and narrows its aims. In particular, the distinction is important in that it identifies the mechanism or the process by which NW is supposed to achieve its aims. NW is primarily geared to detecting crime and deterring offenders. It is not designed to create villages in cities or to socialise resident criminals into more law-abiding modes of behaviour.

The Development of NW in Britain

The idea of NW stems from the early experimental schemes conducted in the United States. In particular, NW is seen as having its origins in the programme implemented in Seattle, Washington in 1973 under the title of the Seattle Community Crime Prevention Programme. NW arrived in Britain along a number of different routes - all of them beginning in North America. The 'Home Watch' scheme implemented in Mollington in Cheshire in June 1982, for example, was the combined result of pressure from the public for the police to do something about burglary rates and the fact that one of the senior officers in Cheshire constabulary had heard about the North American experiments. Similarly, the 'Community Watch' Programme implemented in South Wales in March 1983 was largely the inspiration of one of the Detective Chief Inspectors of the South Wales Constabulary who had recently held a Churchill Fellowship which involved visiting the United States and preparing a paper on Community Watch programmes.

The Development of NW in London

The history of NW in London begins in October 1982 with the appointment of Sir Kenneth Newman as Commissioner of the Metropolitan Police. On his first day in office, The Times published an article outlining the new Commissioner's interest in NW as part of an overall plan to promote proactive policing (The Times, 1982). On 6 September 1983, less than a year following the Commissioner's appointment, NW was launched in London on a forcewide basis.

An important event in the development of NW in London was the publication early in 1983 of a report by Superintendent Turner and Detective Inspector Barker who had recently returned from a study tour of the United States of America to investigate the workings of NW programmes in selected parts of the country. The report represented the first major policy document issued by the Met. and included, along with a descriptive summary of schemes in Washington, D.C., New York, Detroit, Seattle and Orlando police departments, a proposal for the implementation of NW in London.

The recommendations of this report were broadly accepted and formed the basis of the Force Instructions which were circulated by the Assistant Commissioner of 'A' Department of 13 June 1983 (Assistant Commissioner 'A' Department, 1983). The Force Instructions and the 'A' Department Memorandum were sent to all divisional chief superintendents along with a request to make plans for the implementation of NW schemes in their areas in preparation for the official forcewide launch later that year. The Force Instructions provided a summary of the main elements of NW and broad guidelines on methods of implementation. Details of the official launch were announced internally on 2 September in Police Order 24 and the official public launch took place at a press conference on 6 September 1983.

What is Neighbourhood Watch?

One method of describing NW is by outlining the principles and
principal elements of the programme as conceived by policy makers.
Because of the author's recent research into NW in the MPD and because
almost one-quarter of all schemes in the country are contained within
its boundaries, the following discussion focusses predominantly on NW
in London.

The primary sources of information concerning the principles of NW in
the Met. are the Turner and Barker report (Turner and Barker, 1983),
the 'A' Department Memorandum including the Force Instructions
(Assistant Commissioner 'A' Department, 1983) and the official guide
to NW (Russell, undated). The three documents are broadly in
agreement about both the principles and the principal elements.

The 'A' Department Memorandum introduced the concept of NW as, '...
primarily a network of public spirited members of the community, who
become the eyes and ears of the police' (1983, p.1). The concept of
the public becoming the 'eyes and ears' of the police is noted in each
of the three policy documents and has been picked up the press and by
crime prevention departments as a convenient catch phrase to summarise
the essence of NW. The Force Instructions elaborate this idea
further. The key section of the Instructions is reproduced below:

> Neighbourhood Watch is primarily a network of public
> spirited members of the community, who observe what is
> going on in their own neighbourhood and report
> suspicious activity to the police. In simple terms the
> citizen becomes the 'eyes and ears' of the police,
> looking out for the usual and unusual to protect their
> own home and that of their neighbour, thereby reducing
> opportunities for criminal activity. (1983, 1)

NW in London is conceived as a comprehensive package. The Force
Instructions describe the package as comprising four elements: (1)
Neighbourhood Watch - as described above; (2) Property Marking Schemes
- which involves participants in the programme marking property
visibly or invisibly with a house number or first two letters of the
house name along with the post code; (3) Home Security Surveys -

whereby the police provide a free home security survey to advise participants on minimum levels of protection and low cost solutions; and (4) Community Crime Prevention and Environmental Awareness - which is described as the promotion of crime prevention and community campaigns to address particular local environmental issues.

The official guidelines add to this list three more elements: (1) Information - attempts to encourage the flow of information traditionally supplied to the police force by the public; (2) Community Spirit - attempts to encourage people to meet together to create an atmosphere in which neighbours are known to one another and are prepared to look after each other's property; and (3) Police-Public Contact - attempts to keep participants aware of local crime trends and to provide advice and other relevant information. The guidelines also describe more clearly than the Force Instructions what is meant by the fourth element 'Environmental Awareness'. The guidelines refer to Environmental Awareness as an attempt: 'to encourage members to consider their surroundings and put forward suggestions regarding alterations and improvements that could remove the opportunity for criminal nuisance e.g.: (1) the addition or re-positioning of street lighting may reduce instances of criminal damage and rowdyism; (2) the re-designing of certain areas may prevent corridors and walkways being used as general thoroughfares and lead to residents noticing strangers.' (Russell, undated, 2). The section is concluded with the caveat: 'It is acknowledged that this is a long term objective and should be linked to a multi-agency involvement'.

NW in London can also be described by looking at the intended structure and operation of the schemes. From the outset it was envisaged that schemes would be both police initiated and public initiated. Originally, a high proportion of the programmes were police initiated, although now, due to public demand and pressures on police time, most schemes are public initiated. The original instructions for police initiated schemes were to target areas with high levels of residential burglary, to divide these areas into manageable sized groups, to canvass the target area by distributing a questionnaire to, residents and to hold a public meeting during which the aims of the scheme were announced. Public initiated schemes were to be encouraged if a core group of 10-15 neighbours willing to support the scheme could be established. It was believed that a large number of these requests would come from members of resident associations and other community groups. During the early period of NW programmes of varying sizes were implemented ranging from just a few households to in excess of 3,000. It is now considered impracticable to manage very small and very large schemes and the optimal size sought is around 300-500 dwellings.

A new NW scheme begins with a public launch meeting. Originally, it was intended that two public meetings should be held within two weeks of one another, although it is now standard practice to hold just one meeting. The guidelines propose that the aims of the launch meeting are to explain the principles of NW, to indicate how the programme operates (supported by a video presentation), to explain property marking and home security surveys, to encourage residents to note and report suspicious incidents to the police, to disseminate information on recorded crime in the area and to explain the roles of the area and street co-ordinators. Once established, providing there is evidence of acceptable levels of participation, street signs will be erected at all entrances to the NW site. Residents are encouraged by their area and street co-ordinators to display window stickers identifying themselves as participants in the scheme.

Apart from the initial launch meeting, it was envisaged that participants would continue to hold regular informal and formal meetings. The formal meetings were to provide an opportunity for additional training of street co-ordinators and were to be held at one of the members' homes. In fact, very few schemes hold regular formal meetings for the benefit of all residents participating in the scheme. Instead, most hold only informal meetings comprising area and street co-ordinators and their invited guests. The aim of these meetings is not, as was originally intended, the short-term training of co-ordinators, but often to create an opportunity for interaction between a selected minority of the programme participants and the police. Unfortunately, the potential benefits of these meetings are not enjoyed by the majority of participants in the scheme.

In addition to holding informal meetings either the police alone or in collaboration with the area and street co-ordinators prepare regular newsletters. The newsletter contains information on local crime trends, security and other advice, and news of local events relevant to the area and is usually distributed by the street co-ordinators to residents within the NW area. Not all schemes, however, prepare newsletters and not all schemes which do prepare them publish them regularly.

What are the aims of NW?

The primary aim of NW as outline in the Force Instructions is to reduce crime and the fear of crime (Assistant Commissioner 'A' Department, 1983, p.1). More specifically, NW is seen as a weapon against 'opportunist crime' (the definition of this is still unclear, see Bennett and Wright, 1984) and in particular residential burglary. In addition, the Force Instructions identify street robbery, vehicle crime and criminal damage as offences that might also be reduced as a result of the successful implementation of NW.

Additional aims are summarised in the guidelines. The full list of aims include: (1) a reduction in crime levels; (2) heightened public awareness of the need to safeguard property; (3) greater contact between neighbours; (4) closer liaison between police and public; (5) a reduction in the fear of crime; and (6) greater participation by members of the public thereby reducing the demand upon the services of police (Russell, undated, p.1).

How does NW achieve its aims?

It is not absolutely clear from the available policy and publicity material available how NW is supposed to achieve these aims. Some processes, however, have been articulated in the literature.

Crime reduction

The main mechanism that can be found in reports cited above which links NW to decreases in crime is 'opportunity reduction'. The most frequently recorded process by which NW is supposed to reduce opportunities is as a result of residents looking out for suspicious activities and reporting these to the police. The logical link between reporting and crime reduction is not elaborated. It might be argued, however, that reporting suspicious incidents to the police will deter offenders as they will be aware of the local residents' propensity to report suspicious behaviour and perceive the probability of getting caught as a result as unacceptable high. It might also be argued that increasing information flow from the public to the police will improve arrest and conviction rates and (when a custodial sentence is passed) decrease the number of active offenders in the area and the number of crimes committed.

Another mechanism which is not mentioned in these reports, but is occasionally mentioned in the publicity material, is the creation of signs of occupancy. It is interesting that the London version of NW, although based to a large extent on the 'Community Crime Prevention Program' in Seattle, has not stressed in the same way the importance of signs of occupancy. Some of the methods that might be used are discussed in Cirel et al (1977) and in Smith (1984) in the guidelines issued by the Home Office and include removing newspapers and milk from outside neighbours' homes when they are away. It could be argued that the mechanism which links signs of occupancy to crime reduction is the effect that such cues have on the perceptions and assessments of potential offenders. Potential offenders might perceive the probability of getting caught in an apparently occupied dwelling as excessive and, as a result, refrain from offending.

The methods by which the other components of the NW package reduce crime is spelt out more fully. The Force Instructions argue that property marking enhances levels of detection and conviction and makes criminal disposal of property more difficult. Presumably, the former would have the effect of decreasing the number of active offenders through increases in arrest rates which, as a result, would decrease crime, and the latter would deter offenders due to an increase in their perceptions of the probability of getting caught. In addition, it is argued that the property marking sticker alone might act as a deterrent to potential offenders, again, presumably, because they would perceive the risks of getting caught in a dwelling with a window sticker displayed or with marked goods as unacceptably high.

The mechanism defined in the literature as linking home security to crime reduction is its preventive effect in relation to 'opportunistic crime'. This could mean one of two things: either the improvement in security is such that open windows or doors no longer motivate the previously unmotivated offender or the improvements in security prevent any but the most highly motivated and experienced offender from entering.

Environmental awareness, the fourth item in the package, is reported as reducing crime again through reductions in opportunities. The guidelines note that repositioning street lighting and redesigning public access routes, for example, might reduce the opportunities for certain kinds of offence largely, it might be assumed, as a result of increasing offenders' estimation of risks of getting caught.

Fear of crime
Fear of crime might be reduced as a result of at least two different processes. It is sometimes argued that fear of crime is highly correlated with area crime rates and a reduction in crime will almost certainly lead to a reduction in fear of crime. It has also been argued that fear of crime can reduce as a direct result of residents' involvement in crime prevention activities. Reductions in fear may arise, for example, as a result of residents coming together and discussing crime problems.

Evaluations of NW: Does it Work?

Britain

Most evaluations of NW currently available in Britain are those conducted by the police involved in setting up the schemes. Most of these evaluations have examined the impact of NW on crime. Almost all of them report that NW has led to reductions in crime - mainly in the offences of burglary and theft of, and from, motor vehicles. Unfortunately, the research suffers from a number of general methodological weaknesses. Without wishing to appear over critical of police evaluations, which on the whole should be encouraged, it is necessary for this review to comment on some of the important methodological weaknesses of this research.

First, police studies are nearly all based on police recorded crimes as their primary source of data. It is now widely recognised, especially since the publication of the two British Crime Surveys, that police recorded crimes exclude a large number of offences and are strongly affected by changes in public reporting and police recording practices. This is a particularly important problem in relation to NW evaluations. One of the stated functions of NW is to increase public reporting of crime. It is possible, therefore, that police recorded crime might increase as a result of a scheme, not because crimes have increased, but because the public are reporting a greater proportion of them.

Second, there is the problem of small numbers. Police evaluations often are conducted in small areas which have lower than average crime rates before the schemes were implemented. An experimental period of one year, or sometimes only six or even three months, results in a very small number of crimes. An evaluation in Northumbria reported a 22% reduction in residential burglary as a result of a reduction from 18 to 14 offences. Even the more dramatic 90% reduction in burglaries reported by the Cheshire Constabulary was the result of a change from only 19 to 2 offences.

Third most of the evaluations comprise simple 'before' - 'after' comparisons with no adequate control area comparisons. This could be overcome to some extent by including figures for the police area as a whole, but even this is often omitted. The reader is left wondering whether changes in the level of crime were greater or less than expected or greater or less than crime in other areas.

Probably the best police evaluation is that based on the Kingsdown NW project in Bristol. The project was based on a comparison of a 12 month period before the initiation of the scheme and a 12 month period following the launch using a postal questionnaire survey of residents in the NW area. The results of the questionnaire analysis revealed a 24% overall reduction in crime. This was matched by an overall increase in crime in the control area.

Overall, police evaluations in Britain show some reduction in the level of crime. But there remains a question mark over their methodological adequacy which makes any general conclusion difficult.

United States of America

Evaluation in the United States have been conducted both by the police and by independent researchers. The police evaluations suffer all of the problems already mentioned in relations to British police research. They are generally favourable and supportive of the concept of NW, but the research methods often suffer from methodological weaknesses. A recent review of some of these reports shows that the overall conclusion is that NW is an overwhelming success with reported reduction in crime during their first year of operation typically between one-third and one-half (Titus, 1984).

The small number of evaluations by independent researchers, however, are generally less encouraging. One of the first and one of the best evaluations of a comprehensive NW programme was conducted in Seattle during 1975 (Cirel et al, 1977). The initial results of the evaluation showed a reduction in residential burglary for participants in the schemes of over 60% during the first 12 months of the scheme.

They found reporting rates to have increased and little evidence of displacement of crime to neighbouring areas or to non-participants. A telephone survey of the residents in the treatment areas 18 months after the implementation of the scheme, however, showed little difference between participants and non-participants in levels of crime. The authors concluded that the initial positive effects of NW might wear off after a period of between 12 and 18 months.

Another independent survey of a community programme which included NW type principles was conducted in Hartford, Connecticut (Fowler et al, 1979). The researchers concluded that in the first two years of operation both burglary and robbery rates reduced significantly. Again, however, a follow-up study two years later revealed no difference between the rates in the experimental area and in the city as a whole.

More recent evaluations in the United States have produced similarly discouraging findings. A study of NW in Washington D.C. found that in the first 6 months of the scheme the number of crimes increased - although in the second 6 month period crimes did begin to decrease. However, during the same period crime in the city as a whole decreased. They found no difference between blocks that were active and blocks that were inactive in terms of reductions in crime (Henig, 1984).

The most surprising findings come from a recently completed evaluation of NW in Chicago. The analysis is based on five community organisations which implemented NW schemes within their areas. The results of a 'before' and 'after comparison of experimental and control areas showed that in three of the five areas their was an overall increase in crime following the implementation of NW. In only one of the five areas was there a decrease in crime. Crime levels in Chicago as a whole over the same period remained stable. In addition the research revealed further negative findings. In three of the five areas there was a significant increase in the fear of crime and in two of the areas residents felt that crime had increased in their area. Optimism about the area declined in three areas and perceived likelihood of moving increased in two areas (Rosenbaum, Lewis and Grant, 1985).

Evaluations of NW: Participation

For NW to be effective, it is not only necessary that it is capable of achieving its aims, but also that it is accepted by residents and widely implemented. Over the last few years, a number of studies have been published, mainly in the United States, on the willingness of communities to take-up neighbourhood crime prevention programmes. The results of the research have been fairly consistent.

One of the major findings to come out of these studies is that there are important differences between participants and non-participants. In particular, participants are more likely than non-participants to be involved in other community organisations. Typical methods of determining this are to ask respondents if they knew of any community groups in their areas, if they could name them, if they had ever been involved with them and if they could describe the activities of the groups and what they stood for (Skogan and Maxfield, 1981). One of the few independent empirical studies of NW in Britain conducted by students at the University of Surrey, showed that over 90% of participants in NW in one of the areas investigated were members of other community organisations: usually residents' or tenants' associations (Bennion et al, 1985).

A related finding which emerges is that participants are also more heavily integrated in their communities than non-participants. Social integration is usually measured in terms of neighbourhood social knowledge measured by the ease with which strangers can be identified and the number of local children known by name, and neighbourhood crime knowledge measured by the number of types of victim known. Sentimental integration is also measured in terms of whether the respondent feels a part of the neighbourhood and expects to live in the neighbourhood in two years' time (DuBow and Podolefsky, 1982).

The research has also found that there are important similarities between participants and non-participants. It has been shown, for example, that participants are no more likely than non-participants to take more security precautions (DuBow and Podolefsky, 1982). Similarly little difference has been found between participants and non-participants in terms of perceptions of crime or beliefs about the efficacy of crime prevention measures.

Reasons for joining neighbourhood crime prevention programmes vary between studies. Studies which have divided reasons into 'private-minded' or 'public-minded' show that collective actions, such as neighbourhood campaigns, are linked to 'public-minded' motives whereas individual actions, such as fitting security devices, are linked to 'private-minded' motives (Lavrakas, 1981). Similar results have come from studies in Britain which have shown a spread of reasons which can be divided into 'individual oriented' and 'community oriented'(Donnison et al. 1986). Other research has shown that reasons for joining neighbourhood programmes often concern the prevention of potential problems from arising in the future (such as higher crime rates) rather than existing problems (Lavrakas and Hertz, 1982). Reasons for not joining neighbourhood schemes are equally wide ranging and have been categorised as 'no time', 'no interest' and 'no opportunity' (Lavrakas and Hertz, 1982). Other studies have reported non-participation as a result of respondents claiming they are 'too busy', 'too old' or 'too sick' as well as evidence of hostility among people towards the police (Donnison et al. 1986).

Evaluations of NW: Impressions, rumours and hypotheses

The literature on NW is scattered with speculative comment comprising anecdotal material, opinion and perceived hazards associated with the implementation of watch programmes. In themselves, these comments do not comprise research evidence. Nevertheless, it is useful to present them as issues which have arisen out of the debate. No attempt has been made to assess the validity of these claims.

A common argument cited against NW is that it is socially divisive. Proponents of this view argue that NW is run by a small unrepresentative section of the community for the benefit of their own social group. The social divisions usually referred to concern social class or income divisions. Some critics have taken this line of argument further to suggest that NW could reinforce race differences and exacerbate racial tensions. Alternatively, it is argued that in an area of racial tension, it is unlikely that people will unite behind a NW scheme. Attempts to promote NW in such areas can leave the police accused of exacerbating or perpetuating social inequalities.

A second criticism linked to the first is the view that the organisers of NW schemes are unrepresentative of the community and attract a disproportionate share of police resources. It is argued, for example, that police resources are drawn into low crime, middle class areas which results in police time being spent in areas which need them least (Donnison et al. 1986). In addition, it is argued that crime prevented in these areas is likely to be displaced into areas less suitable for NW which in turn reinforces socio-economic inequalities.

A third criticism concerns the level of police control over NW programmes. It is argued that the public and the police might hold different perceptions of the nature of the problems in an area. For example, residents might be most concerned about people loitering in the streets, graffiti and noise from neighbours, whereas the police might wish to focus community attention on the problem of residential burglary. A linked criticism is that some residents might object to any king of involvement of the police in the community including community efforts to prevent crime.

A fourth problem presented by many commentators, including the police, is the fear that NW might promote vigilantism. It is official policy in the Met. that NW should not include citizen patrols and the existence of these or similar programme elements should be rigorously discouraged. It has been argued, however, that not all police share this view and some will allow patrols (Donnison et al. 1986).

Other criticisms include the view that NW encourages neighbours to spy on each other which can break rather than restore communities. It is feared the specific groups or specific individuals within the group will be selected out for special treatment and become ostracised. It is also feared that this selection might be based on stereotypical expectations of the behaviour of individuals or groups.

Summary

The paper has drawn attention to a number of issues concerning the definition, operation and evaluation of NW. It has been argued that watch schemes have evolved from the situational approach and the mechanism by which NW aims to reduce crime is through opportunity reduction. Evaluations of the effect of NW on crime have been conducted by both the police and by independent researchers. The research has produced mixed findings: police evaluations have tended to produce more favourable results and independent evaluations have tended to produce less favourable results. Evaluations of the take up of neighbourhood crime prevention programmes have shown important differences between participants and non-participants suggesting that such schemes are not universally supported or universally appropriate as measures to prevent crime. Anecdotal evidence and general comment has focussed on the perceived negative consequences of NW and the unwanted effects that such schemes might have on community structures.

References

Assistant Commissioner 'A' Department (1983), Neighbourhood Watch
    Schemes Memorandum issued 13 June along with the document Force
    Instructions: Neighbourhood Watch, 'A' Department, Metropolitan
    Police.

Bennett T.H. and Wright R. (1984), Burglars on Burglary: Prevention and the Offender, Aldershot: Gower.

Bennion C., Dawe A., Hesse B.H., Joshua L., McGloin P., Munn G. and Tester S. (1985), Neighbourhood Watch: The Eyes and Ears of Urban Policing? Occasional Papers in Sociology and Social Policy No. 6, Surrey: Department of Sociology, University of Surrey.

Cirel P., Evans P., McGillis D. and Whitcomb D. (1977), Community Crime Prevention, Seattle, Washington: An Exemplary Project. Washington D.C.: LEAA, U.S. Department of Justice, Government Printing Office.

Clarke, R.V.G. (1980), 'Situational Crime Prevention: Theory and Practice', British Journal of Criminology, Vol. 20, pp.136-147.

Donnison H., Scola J. and Thomas P. (1986), Neighbourhood Watch: Policing the People, London: The Libertarian Research and Education Trust.

DuBow F. and Podolefsky A. (1982), 'Citizen Participation in Community Crime Prevention', Human Organization, Vol. 41, pp.307-314.

Fowler F.J., McCalla M.E. and Mangine T.W. (1979) Reducing Residential Crime and Fear: The Hartford Neighbourhood Crime Prevention Program, Washington D.C.: Government Printing Office.

Henig J.R. (1984), Citizens Against Crime: An Assessment of the Neighbourhood Watch Program in Washington, D.C., Occasional Paper No. 2, Centre for Washington Area Studies, Washington, D.C.: George Washington University.

Lavrakas, P.J. (1981), Factors Related to Citizen Involvement in Personal, Household and Neighbourhood Anti-Crime Measures. Washington, D.C.: National Institute of Justice.

Lavrakas P.L. and Hertz E.J. (1982), 'Citizen Participation in
    Neighbourhood Crime Prevention', Criminology, Vol. 20, No. 3,
    pp.479-498.

Rosenbaum D.P., Lewis D.A. and Grant J.A. (1985), The Impact of
    Community   Crime   Prevention   Programs   in   Chicago: Can
    Neighbourhood Organization Make A Difference? Final Report:
    Volume One, Northwestern University: Center for Urban Affairs
    and Policy Research.

Russell J. (Undated), A Guide to Neighbourhood Watch Schemes, 'A'
    Department, Metropolitan Police.

Shaw C.R. and McKay H.D. (1969), Juvenile Delinquency and Urban Areas,
    Chicago: University of Chicago Press.

Skogan W.G. and Maxfield M.G. (1981), Coping with Crime, London: Sage.

Smith L.J.F. (1984), Neighbourhood Watch: A Note on Implementation,
    London: Home Office Crime Prevention Unit.

Titus R. (1984), 'Residential Burglary and the Community Response', in
    Clarke R.V.G. and Hope T. (eds), Coping with Burglary, Boston:
    Kluwer-Nijhoff.

The Times (1982), 'The Very Model Chief of the Omnicompetent
    Constable', The Times, 2 October, London: Times Newspapers Ltd.

Turner B.W.M. and Barker P.J. (1983), Study Tour to the United States
    of America: 7th March 1983 to 21st March 1983, Volumes 1 and 2,
    Metropolitan Police.

THE SPECIAL CONSTABULARY:

COMMUNITY REPRESENTATIVES AND ACCOUNTABILITY

M L Gill

Research Officer

Centre for Criminology and Criminal Justice

University of Hull

Introduction

Despite the growing volumes of literature on policing, and much of it focusing on police and community relation, remarkably little has been written on the special constabulary. In many ways their omission is difficult to comprehend, since specials as they are known, are members of the public who volunteer their services to act as police officers for about 4 hours per week. Ostensibly, the specials are a reserve force should some disaster delete the regular establishment, and the duties and training in which they engage are preparation for that eventuality. At the same time it is recognised that they are in an ideal position to forge links between the police and the community and foster harmony in an interchange which is continually under stress. Surprisingly though, just as specials have been neglected by academics, both in the volunteer and policing literature, so too they appear to have been much neglected as reserve by senior officers.

Recently the Home Office has taken initiatives to advice chief constables of the need to increase the number of special constables (Home Office, 1986). Certainly crime prevention projects such as neighbourhood watch have marked an obvious area for their greater utilisation (e.g. Newton, 1987; Veater, 1984a; 1984b). Previously a role had been seen for specials in being attached to community beat officers to provide them with knowledge and contacts in the local community (Alderson, 1978). However, very little is known about what specials do in practice. True, in the mid 1970s the Police Advisory Board for Scotland set up a working party on the specials, which reported in 1975. Then the following year the Police Advisory Board for England and Wales reported on its research into the special constabulary (Police Advisory Board, 1976), and this was supplemented by a second report five years later (Police Advisory Board, 1981). It is these reports which form the basis for official policy on the special constabulary today.

Certainly, the reports proposed sweeping changes, including the expectation of a minimum and regular commitment; a specified training programme; and perhaps more controversially, a change in the ranking structure to differentiate them from the regulars. In their reports the Advisory Boards could only make recommendations, and as such the extent to which these and other changes were implemented remains unknown. The object of the study discussed here was to evaluate the role of the specials in one force, and supplement the work by visits to other constabularies. The research was part of a much wider project into the role of the volunteers in the criminal justice system which has been reported elsewhere (Gill, 1986; Mawby and Gill, 1987) and it is anticipated that more detailed discussions will follow in ensuing publications. The object here is merely to review some of the more salient findings.

Ignorance abounds on the type of people who become specials. Historically, specials have been seen as having a distinctive place in the class structure (Seth, 1961; Whitaker, 1979), and one writer, without citing evidence, has claimed that they are recruited from the petit bourgeoisie (Bunyan, 1977). On the other hand, when the class background of regular officers was researched by Reiner (1978; 1982), this revealed the class similarity of regular officers to the general population. What is striking as Table 1 illustrates, is that despite the scepticism of some, specials - at least in the South West - are drawn from similar class groupings to regulars.

TABLE 1

Reiner's (1978, p.150) Table of the Social Class Background
of Police and Social Composition of Population with Class Details
on Specials Added[1]

Registrar General's Class	1971 Census %	Police Officers %	Specials %
I	4.9	2.4	3.9
II	19.8	14.9	23.6
III	49.0	53.6	49.8
IV	18.6	19.1	17.0
V	7.7	3.6	5.7
NA	-	6.5	-
Manual	61.1	59.6	52.4
Non Manual	38.9	34.0	38.9

Quite clearly the similarities are extremely marked. It is also interesting that the special constabulary, unlike most groups of volunteers (Aves, 1969) does not have a predominantly middle class bias. What though of ideology? During the Devon and Cornwall research question were incorporated into the Interview Schedule on attitudes to law and order, sentencing practice and voting behaviour. The object here was to see if there was any link between social class, and attitudes, and how this related to the official and unofficial ideology of the organisational. In the case of the police for example, there has since 1979 and the election of a Conservative government on a law and order ticket been a close link between the political right and the police.

Interestingly, although the specials were considerably less likely to be middle class than either probation voluntary associates or victims support scheme volunteers, they were more likely to have harsher attitudes to law and order, favour tougher sentences, and vote Conservative. In other words, just as specials, like police officers, appear to be representative of the general public in terms of class background, they also appear to identify with the political right (for a fuller discussion see Gill, 1986).

If some sort of similarity can be found between the specials and the public in terms of social class backgrounds, the same is not true in terms of gender and ethnic minority presence.[2] The specials were predominantly male. However, two points are worth noting here. First, the number of women in the special constabulary is twice that in the regular establishment. This was found to be the case in both the research force as well as nationally. Second, the majority of **applicants** to the specials in the research force were found to be women which supports the findings of Hope and Boyd (1984) in their study of the metropolitan police. In fact, 1982 marked the first occasion in thirty years that the numbers in the special constabulary nationally had increased, and this was due entirely to the growing participation of women.

In terms of age, specials were represented across a range of age groupings, although there was a tendency for them to be slightly younger than the population mean. In many respects therefore, the stereotype typical volunteer as described by Aves (1969) as a middle aged, middle class married women, would be wholly inapplicable to specials.

These results are interesting if only because they dispel some traditional myths, but they are of greater significance in the context of accountability, a popular concept in present discussions of policing. It has been well documented that the police have considerable discretion in the lower ranks, and part of the problem for advocates of increased accountability is how to ensure fairness without prohibiting the use of discretion. The Police and Criminal Evidence Act 1984, introduced in January 1986 was an attempt to regulate police behaviour through the issuing of strict guidelines and codes of practice. Cynics however have argued that the effects are likely to be minimal because the legislation is misconceived in assuming that police officers are guided by legal rules (Smith, 1986). One alternative therefore is to make police work more visible; the introduction of lay visitors is seen as an important development here, although clearly the amount of work to which visitors are likely to have access is small. The same is not true however of specials who accompany officers in their daily tasks but are still members of the community. Hence, could a greater use of the specials increase the visibility of the police and as such render the organisation more accountable?

Prima facie evidence would suggest there is much to commend such a viewpoint. It has been shown already that specials are not unlike regular officers in terms of background and political or ideological attitudes. This is important because of the much discussed police subculture which brings with it a suspicion of outsiders (Holdaway, 1983). The police sub-culture has a number of tennets, but central values include the support of colleagues in the face of adversity. As the Policy Studies Institute's research recently concluded:

> "We were told many times that an officer who had done something wrong would always, or almost always, be backed up by other officers, even if they didn't like him" (Smith and Gray, 1983; p.71)

Now, given that specials are volunteers, community representatives as it were, it may be expected that they would bring to wider attention any transgression of guidelines. Conversely, as police officers they would be expected to support colleagues in pursuit of police objectives; as such this may entail "backing up" officers when something had been done incorrectly. How, then, does this apparent contradiction resolve itself in practice?

Perhaps a starting point along the road to answering this question would be to consider the type of work specials undertake, and to what extent they are involved in working with regular officers and then their perceived view of the special/regular partnership. This indeed has been the subject of some considerable comment, with Police Review bristling with correspondence on the antipathy of regular officers towards specials.[3]

The Police Advisory Board's (1976) observation that specials tended to work alongside regular officers was confirmed by two thirds of respondents, although just under half the remainder claimed they were equally likely to work with a regular as with a special. Even those specials who claimed that they usually worked with other specials said that they did occasionally accompany regulars. No special usually patrolled alone, although this did sometimes happen.

There was little evidence that specials attached themselves to community police officers as Alderson (1978) had envisaged. Indeed those specials who accompanied regular officers noted that it was normally a different officer each time. When out, specials tended to either double up and act as an observer in a panda car, or attend on foot patrol. Work on traffic duty or crowd control particularly at events such as carnivals, fetes, or football matches was also common. Some officers even managed to gain access to departments like CID, but this was rare and depended on them knowing the people concerned. In a similar context the number of hours specials committed varied, although nearly 30% claimed to undertake more than the recommended maximum of 4 hours per week.

By all accounts then, specials were in a position, via a mixture of observation and experience, to monitor and comment on the work of uniformed officers. So what was their view of regular officers, and as importantly, what were regular officers' view of them?[4] During the interviews specials were asked four questions, to which they were invited to respond on a scale ranging from 'very favourable' to 'very unfavourable'. They were asked to state the attitudes of police officers to themselves and their own attitude to the officers with whom they worked. Then their opinion was sought on the attitude of police officers to specials generally, and of other specials towards police officers.

The specials thought very highly of regular officers, and believed this to be reciprocated. There were very few negative comments; indeed the main level of interest was whether the emphasis was on the 'very favourable' or the 'favourable' category. This was true of all four questions. Nobody answered 'very unfavourable' at all, although one special considered the attitudes of regulars was 'unfavourable' on a personal level, and 3 did so when considering regulars' views generally. Amongst these answers, and even those who answered with 'indifferent', were those who maintained the threat specials potentially pose to regulars overtime was real. For example:

> "I think they are anti. They believe we are taking duties from them when they could be paid overtime for taking those duties." (SC06)

> "I think they think we are taking their overtime, that is the long and short of it." (SC44)

Still, positive comments were in abundance, and sometimes this boarded on admiration. For example:

> "I look up to the officer." (SC28)

> "A great bunch of blokes with a bloody difficult job to do." (SC48)

Many specials reflected that their own perceived popularity derived from the fact that they released officers from tasks in which they would not want to be engaged, such as carnivals and fetes. Others pointed out the benefits to regular officers in being 'double crewed' and having company. Some specials, however, considered the attitude of specials to be crucial, ensuring that they did not overstep into the professionals' domain. For example:

> "I get on with 95% of them because I don't push myself. If they ask me to do something I do it. If they don't I shut up." (SC07)

"They seem friendly, we don't step on their toes, in
fact we stand back and do what we are told." (SC10)

In all specials saw their main role as assisting police officers, as a
back up service. Indeed, only 15.7% had individually made an arrest
(over a quarter had never been involved in arresting anyone) with many
specials claiming that when accompanying regular officers it was the
latter who did the work, specials usually being just support should
difficulties arise.

So specials considered that they were highly regarded by police
officers and that to a certain extent this was dependent upon
specials' attitude, particularly in recognising the professionals'
dominant role. Nevertheless, they regarded the officers highly. But
what happens when specials witness a transgression of guidelines by
regulars?

The answer to this question was gleaned from casual conversation with
specials, where the consistency of replies received was striking.
Specials like police officers derived most satisfaction from being
involved in 'real police work' (Cain, 1973), such as car chases,
fights, or even arrests. For specials such events were rare, although
because of this, when they did occur they were accentuated in
importance, frequently marking a milestone in a special's career. In
such incidents their role as a support was heightened, and it was a
role they took very seriously indeed. The following example reflects
one special's experience which was retold to an audience of special
colleagues and the researcher:

> "I was out on one occasion with a group of officers,
> quite a few of us there were, when we came across a
> bunch of yobs. They were a bit hippy and we realised we
> would have to do something about it. So we began to
> argue (with them) a bit. Then one police constable,
> standing away from us all, bent over pretending to have
> been thumped. He hadn't of course, but we had so many
> statements saying he had been hit it was incredible.
> Anyway, we had the yobs, it was a good night."

As far as the specials were concerned the rules had been broken, but
that had been necessary to detain "yobs". There were countless other

examples of similar type incidents. The point is not that specials were keen to flaunt the law: they certainly were not. Rather, where bending of the rules was necessary to apprehend offenders, specials shared with the regulars a perception of what was permissible.

There was thus a strong tendency for specials to see situations from the police angle, and there was certainly a reluctance to state that they would report officers for misdemeanours, although some said they would. Part of the problem though is that any report would require corroboration. In any event whereas examples of where specials had witnessed and supported a bending of rules were common, examples of specials reporting officers were extremely rare. Specials saw their role as helping the police, they shared with them similar views on law and order and policing, and wanted to be involved in the daily activities of the police. Many specials noted that if one of them was to break the 'secrecy code' then it would reflect badly not only on the individual, but on the special constabulary as a whole.

It is important not to exaggerate this issue. Infractions of the law were rare, as specials emphasised, and the work of police officers was much admired by the volunteers. On the one hand cynics may contend that their opinions are tainted with their pro-police posture, but had they considered regular officers to be consistently breaking rules there would be much scope for concern. Instead, specials considered regulars to be conscientious. The problem is though, that for advocates of greater visibility of police work via increased use of the specials, the pro-police perspectives of specials is crucial. But how does this situation arise?

The answer probably lies in a mixture of motivations, selection policies and training programmes. Volunteers in the study were asked two questions regarding their motivations. First, what initially made them want to do voluntary work, and second, what made them choose the organisation they did. The responses were interesting in that they illuminated the greater interest of specials in the organisation, compared with other groups of volunteers. Twice as many specials as voluntary associates and victims support scheme volunteers claimed their initial reason to volunteer was prompted by a specific interest in the organisation. Moreover, when asked why they joined the agency they did, 58.3% of specials claimed an interest in the organisation, compared to only 36.8 % of voluntary associates and 38.2% of victims support scheme volunteers specials then had a particular interest in the police and policework.

Most specials first heard about the special constabulary from a regular or special, in other words a police source. Some had applied to the regulars and failed or were too old. As such, being accepted as a special was something of a consolation prize. The point though, is that there was quite a high interest in the service and its work. Identity with the police is built upon through the selection procedures which are quite rigorous. This includes in the research force, the sitting of the Police Critical Recruitment Test and the expectation of a pass mark an applicant to the regulars would require, as well as a lengthy home interviews and the provision of two good references.[5] While physical requirements are relaxed for the specials, they are only accepted if they have no criminal records. The whole process can take up to six months and longer to complete. Only the most committed specials pass, and only those the police consider suitable.

Thus only highly committed and motivated people finds themselves in a position to commence training as a special. The frequency of training varies, but is normally held weekly through the winter months along the lines suggested by the Police Advisory Boards Report (1981). There has been much discussion of the relevance of training in the context of volunteers, much of it quibbling as to whether words such as 'preparations' might be more appropriate (See Aves, 1969) although there is little to suggest that it means anything different in practice. Discussions such as these have also tended to distract attention away from important points about volunteer training. For example, much has been written about the need of volunteers the need of volunteers to have some skills via training in order to pursue their task effectively. Rather less has been written on the effect of training in inculcating a sub-culture, something that has been seen as crucial for regular officers. Banton for example has argued:

> "One of the things he acquires at the training centre is a sense of solidarity with his classmates and that policemen must help one another in dealings with the public. He cannot accept ideas which entail disloyalty towards his colleagues." (Banton, 1973, 114)

The same is also true of specials. Lecturers were police officers and thus they were able to explain policing in theory and practice. The use of police vocabulary further helped to build up an identity with the police: specials could learn the police ways. This was reinforced during socialisation periods after training sessions when many specials would retire to the police bar to talk about policework. This combination of a keen interest in the police service initially, maintained through rigorous selection procedures, training and socialisation, results in a member of the public being completely conversant with the police ways, and familiar with police expectations for them. Not surprisingly then that specials share with the police very similar perspectives.

Summary

This paper commenced with a consideration of the social class backgrounds of specials. Here it was shown that like regular officers, similarities with the public at large are quite marked. This did not hold true in respect of gender although there was a higher percentage of women in the specials than in the regular police. The special is very different to the stereotype volunteer, suggesting that greater scrutiny of the special constabulary may vastly improve our knowledge of voluntarism.

Specials are engaged in a wide variety of tasks working for the most part alongside regulars. They are exposed to the daily experiences of police officers. Some specials were able to cite instances where they had witnessed officers circumventing guidelines and even acting illegally. Nevertheless, rather than viewing such transgressions as malignant there was a tendency to see them as essential or inevitable in the pursuit of police objectives. The specials closely identified with the police perspective, this was revealed via a variety of attitudinal questions. They saw things the police way.

For specials to play a role of public eyes in the police it would be necessary for them to view their role as volunteers first and foremost rather than police officers. Such could be achieved through changing the selection procedure, training programme or role, which all help to build up this identity with the service. However, I have argued elsewhere that in practice such policies would be unrealistic. Specials are able to identify with the police and access their subculture, if this was to be threatened it is possible the special constabulary could be isolated altogether.

To a certain extent therefore the role of specials in making the police more accountable is limited. However, this needs to be assessed in context and balanced appropriately. Whilst some may reject totally the role specials can play in the context of accountability, to do so, although perhaps justifiable, in no way distracts from the important role specials adopt in supporting regular officers, not least in relieving them for more demanding tasks. Specials are an extra resource, of benefit to both police and public. Moreover, there is a case for arguing that at least the act of having volunteers in the police service forces the police to think about their role in the community.

Like other groups of volunteers working in state agencies, specials are a much neglected part of organisational policy. They are frequently frowned upon by regulars who appear to misinterpret their intentions and delude themselves of the constabulary's potential in expanding police work in the community. There are signs that things are changing, but a stronger police commitment is essential. For the academic, the special is a much neglected topic. Their role as atypical volunteers and part-time police officer, makes them an interesting topic for study, in both the volunteer and policing worlds.

Footnotes

1. The data on personal characteristics were collected from a sample of records retained by the police. When these were compared with identical data obtained from interviews the similarities were quite marked.

2. Due to the low representation of ethnic minorities in the area covered by the research force, no comment can be made on this point. Certainly, since Scarman's (1981) report there has been considerable discussion on the utilisation of the special constabulary as a mechanism for involving minorities in police work.

3. Most of these ideas have been developed in Gill (1986). However, for more information on this point see Note 14 p.92.

4. The views of regular officers were researched via a postal questionnaire. They were generally favourable. However, due to the limitation of space it is not possible to discuss the results in detail here.

5. The election process varied between divisions, it is discussed in more detail in Gill (1986).

References

Alderson J. (1978) Concepts of Preventive Policing. The Cranfield Papers: the proceedings of the 1978 Cranfield Conference on the prevention of crime in Europe, Peel Press.

Aves G. (1969) The Voluntary Worker in the Social Services. The
        Bedford Square Press of the NCSS and George Allen and Unwin,
        London.

Banton M. (1973) Police Community Relations, William Collins and
        Sons, London.

Bunyan T. (1977) The Political Police in Britain, Quartly Books,
        London.

Cain M. (1973) Society and the Policeman's Role, Routledge and Kegan
        Paul, London.

Gill M.L. (1986) Voluntarism and the Criminal Justice System: A
        Comparative Analysis, Ph.D Thesis, Plymouth Polytechnic.

Holdaway S. (1983) Inside the British Police: A Force at Work, Basil
        Blackwell, Oxford.

Home Office (1986) Criminal Justice: A Working Paper, Home Office,
        London.

Hope A. and Lloyd T. (1984) Increase Recruitment to the MSC,
        Metropolitan Police.

Newton N. (1987) A Special Kind of Watch, Police Review, 27th
        February.

Police Advisory Board for Scotland (1975) Report of the Working
        Party on Special Constables, Scotland.

Police Advisory Board for England and Wales (1976) Report of the
        Working Party on the Special Constabulary.

Police Advisory Board for England and Wales (1981) Report on the
        Second Working Party of the Special Constabulary.

Police Review

Reiner R. (1978)   The Blue-Coated Worker, Cambridge University Press,
        Cambridge.

Reiner R. (1985)   The Politics of the Police, Wheatsheaf Books,
        Brighton.

Scarman, Lord (1981)   Chairman, The Brixton Disorders 10-12 April
        1981, Cmnd 8427, HMSO, London.

Seth R. (1961)   The Specials, Victor Gollancz, London.

Smith D.J. (1986)   The Framework of Law and Policing Practice, in
        Benyon J. and Bourn C. (eds) The Police: Powers, Procedures and
        Properties, Pergamon Press, Oxford.

Smith D.J. and Gray J. (1983)   Police and People in London, Part IV,
        The Police in Action, Policy Studies Institute, London.

Veater P. (1984)   Evaluation of Kingsdown Neighbourhood Watch Project,
        Avon and Somerset Constabulary, Bristol.

Veater P. (1984)   Citizens Against Crime, Police Review, 31st August.

Whitaker B. (1979)   The Police in Society, Eyre Methuen, London.

OCCUPATIONAL SEGREGATION AND WOMEN IN THE POLICE

G Kelland

Research Assistant

Plymouth Polytechnic

Introduction

This paper is drawn from a study, funded by Leverhulme Trust, of the
determinants and consequences of the relatively high wastage rate of
women police officers. A postal survey was administered to all women
constables in two provincial forces from which the response rates were
64 and 50 per cent respectively. In addition, in-depth interviews
were conducted with a follow-up sample of 24 currently serving female
officers and 27 women who had left the job over a three year period;
17 male officers were also interviewed.

To some extent, the careers of women in the police appear to be
constrained by the operation of both ideological and structural
factors which result in a sexual division of labour within the job.
This paper will examine the origins of this division, its consequences
for deployment decisions and its reinforcement by an occupational
culture stressing the dangerous aspects of the job and its definition

as 'men's work'. The division is also buttressed by the myth of women's lack of commitment to police work whereby they are thought to use it as no more than an interlude between school and having children.

The sexual division of labour in the workforce

At about the same time that Peel was establishing the Metropolitan Police in 1929, working women were coming to be regarded as a 'social problem'. Fears were expressed not only about the impact of their working in mines and factories on reproduction and family life, but also the danger of 'moral and spiritual degradation' to which they were exposed (Oakley, 1981). Living and working conditions for working class women contrasted sharply with the growing ideology of domesticity and care of the family as women's 'natural' and primary responsibilities, and the ensuing legislation was to reinforce and extend the sexual division of labour in the workplace. Women and children were no longer to work underground following the Mines Act 1842, and their hours of factory work were restricted in the Factory Act 1844.

There was no intention to exclude women from the labour market, particularly since they provided a cheap source of labour; "it was rather that only those sorts of work that coincided with a woman's natural sphere were to be encouraged" (Alexander, 1976, 62).

Thus there was, for instance, an increase in domestic service for working class women and in the manufacturing sector they were generally confined to 'women's work' which tended to be 'unskilled, overcrowded and low paid'. This division of labour was further reinforced by the active exclusion of women and cheap labour from skilled jobs begun in craft guilds, extended with the growth of trade unionism in the nineteenth century and supported by the ideology of the 'male breadwinner' and female dependency encompassed in the demands for a 'family wage'.

The falling birth rate, high infant mortality rate and the health of the workforce were matters of concern in the latter half of the century, particularly when competition from foreign powers was threatening British profits. It was fertile ground for the ideas of social imperialists concerned for national efficiency. Emphasis was placed on children as a 'national asset' and the ignorance and negligence of working mothers were the focus of attention as the cheap and easy solution to the problem (Davin, 1978). For middle class women, who were not rearing children themselves, work was available in the burgeoning careers of health visiting, teaching and social work "justified ideologically by their greater suitability; it also made the new provisions less expensive" (Davin, 1978, 51).

Thus, there developed in the nineteenth century a pattern of occupational concentration which has persisted to the present day. Women are overrepresented in about a quarter of all occupations in terms of their participation rate in the labour market; men on the other hand are overrepresented in three-quarters of all jobs (Hakim, 1979). Even where women and men are employed in the same occupations, men tend to occupy the higher grade, more skilled and better paid posts. Hakim referred to the former as horizontal segregation and the latter as vertical segregation and found the position had not altered a great deal since 1901. Whilst the equal pay and sex discrimination legislation of the 1970s resulted in progress for some women into 'men's work', especially professional and managerial posts, the effect had since declined probably due to the recession (Hakim, 1981). In the more recent 'Women and Employment Survey', over half of the sample of working women said they were employed on work performed solely by women in their workplace and only 34 per cent were doing types of jobs on which both women and men were engaged (Martin and Roberts, 1984).

Women in the police are an interesting case from the point of view of occupational segregation since they are employed in a job traditionally defined as 'men's work' which is relatively secure and well paid, in comparison to many jobs typically thought of as 'women's work'. The remainder of this paper will show, however, that they are to some extent subject to intra-occupational segregation.

Women for work in the police

The origins of policewomen may be traced to the women's suffrage and 'purity' campaigns of the 1880s when a plethora of pressure groups called upon the Home Secretary to take steps to prevent child prostitution and 'white slave traffic' to the Continent. The pioneers of women police were members of such groups. They were to some extent urged on to participate, it seems, by the lack of activity on the part of the police when legislation was introduced to raise the age of consent to 16 years and they were empowered to remove young children from houses used by prostitutes.

> "There were those in the LNA (Ladies' National Association), the NUWW (National Union of Women Workers) and the women members of the NVA (National Vigilance Association) who argued that a more coercive approach by the police was essential for the protection of 'innocent women and children'" (Mort, 1986, 221).

The social upheaval of the First World War provided the opportunity for the setting up of voluntary women patrols designed, it was made clear, to complement the work of men in the police. As in the fields of health visiting and social work, it was their qualities as women which were emphasised as making them uniquely suitable for controlling prostitution near army camps, enforcing factory regulations with respect to the many women brought into the labour force to manufacture munitions, searching and escorting women prisoners, protecting children and so on.

It was the intention of these early policewomen that, having proven their worth in wartime, they would have a case for being permanently included in the police service when normal conditions returned. However, emphasis on their capacity for specialist work meant that for the most part they remained outside the mainstream of policing, associated with a subsidiary role - 'women's work'. Their hours were shorter than those worked by policemen and their pay was less, and even at the outbreak of the Second World War there were only 119 women police, three-quarters of whom were not attested. The vast majority of forces employed no women officers at all.

Their numbers increased after 1939, war again proving significant in their development, but the role for many remained restricted to work in totally separate Policewomen's Departments until the 1970s. This did tend to vary depending on supervisors and where the women were stationed. In rural areas they often performed the same duties as their male colleagues and there were a few women in specialist posts like Traffic and CID. Despite this, on the whole, they tended to be associated with 'women's work' and not 'real police work' and this connection has had repercussions for how women have been perceived since they have been fully integrated with men in the service.

Opposition to integration

The Policewomen's Department in the Metropolitan Police had already been disbanded in 1972, but for most women officers integration followed the inclusion of the police within the terms of the Sex Discrimination Act 1975. Opposition to integration was expressed by both women and men in the job. Some women complained about the shifts, now they were expected to work at night (although there had been a call-out system for women officers previously) and the fact that they had joined to perform a specialist role and not general patrol work.

Some male officers too preferred women in their specialist capacity and were doubtful about their ability to do general police work, arguing that their lack of physical strength would endanger not only the women but also their male colleagues who would feel bound to protect them. Indeed, one leaver in this survey spoke of policemen protecting women officers as they would their wives. Men were anxious that equality in recruitment would lead to a greater proportion of policewomen and an imbalance therefore in the officers available to cope with dangerous and violent work. Physical differences between women and men may be used in this way to justify their exclusion from certain jobs and physical strength arguments were still prevalent amongst both women and men interviewed in the present study. But, as Hilton (1975, 97) points out, they are arguments only tenable in extreme conditions:

> "In the early stages of potentially violent situations and in all other aspects of crowd control the presence of policewomen may help to reduce the extent to which the situation is seen as a challenging confrontation of male aggression."

One of the leavers interviewed agreed with this:

> "Whenever anyone says to me that policewomen can't cope physically, I always say, well, 90 per cent of the time they don't need to because they defuse a situation which might otherwise have gone on and lead to violence. A policewoman walking into a situation is no threat, whereas a policeman walks in - there's the old aggression comes into it."

Sherman (1973) has written of the 'self-fulfilling prophecy' in some police-public interactions where potentially violent situations may be exacerbated by the expectations people bring to them. On the whole, members of the public do not expect policewomen to behave aggressively and this probably accounts for the media attention paid to the use of female officers in riot situations (see, for example, The Guardian 21.2.86; 14.2.86). As one currently serving policewoman commented:

> "... but then, a lot of men like a bit of violence ... and you'll find it's the same men. People say to a couple of them there, 'You always seem to be where there's trouble.' But I think sometimes the person creates the trouble."

The leaver quoted above had not actually come across the other '10 per cent' of the job - the violent situations which cannot be defused by the mere presence of a policewoman - which is probably not surprising since studies have shown that much of the time, policing is concerned with service, as well as law-enforcement functions. Punch (1983, 102), for instance, has written of the organisation as a 'secret social service' because of the 'grey area' in which police officers are often involved - with "the drunk, the delinquent, the homeless, the drug addict, the problem family, the immigrant, the battered wife". But reality is to some extent unimportant in the argument because the ideology within the occupational culture is formed through selective definitions of police work, and in terms of its crime-fighting role. Speaking of their preference for CID work, two of the men interviewed said:

> "I think because you don't have to deal quite so much with the trivia and you get jobs that you can take a bit of enquiry into - bit of a sort of challenge to crack them."

> "Well, basically, you don't get any rubbish jobs. At the end of the day, a lot of panda work is moving people off yellow lines and jobs like that which I consider are small and menial. They've got to be done, but I don't want to be doing it really."

Hence the feeling that a move from CID to uniform patrol, although lateral, is in some ways a demotion, despite the emphasis from management that beat work is all important.

Arguments about the danger of general police work for women also ignore the fact that policewomen were, and are, liable to assaults from women whilst performing jobs perceived as appropriate for them. The debate about women's physical ability does take on an added significance, however, when used to justify their unequal recruitment. A report in the Guardian (1.11.83) quoted researchers from the Policy Studies Institute study of the Metropolitan Police (Smith and Gray, 1983) who discovered that the numbers of women were being kept at an unofficial quota of 10 per cent:

> "We find that there is a great deal of prejudice against women in the force. It is possible to argue that a substantial increase in the number of women police officers would help to overcome some current problems and would increase the pool of certain resources that are currently scarce within the force."

This is hardly likely, however, given the following, taken from the Sunday Telegraph (8.6.86):

> "'The applicants,' said one Deputy Chief Constable, 'are about 40 per cent female, and, since we only choose 10 per cent, there must be some male chauvinism. You just know that if you tell the divisional commander of a tough area that all his new recruits are female, he'll

say, "Thanks, that's really solved my problems", so subconsciously you tell yourself "We'll recruit one in ten".'"

Opportunities for women in the police

Another criticism levelled at policewomen at the time of integration, and since, has been their tendency to leave after serving only a few years, and the belief that the wastage was generally due to childrearing. In this respect policewomen are, like most other women, still expected to take the primary responsibility for childcare when they have families. The expectation of their domestic role, real or otherwise, then looms large in their prospects for specialisation or promotion. The onus is on female officers to prove their commitment and ambition since, often, the taken-for-granted assumption is that they will leave prematurely and any investment in their careers is therefore wasted. The implication of this stereotyping is that all women are less committed to their jobs whether they intend to leave or not, which is not a problem peculiar to the police service (see for example Homans, 1987, who has written about the myths surrounding women scientists working in the National Health Service).

The present study found that although childbearing and rearing accounted for two-thirds of the wastage amongst those leavers interviewed, 9 out of 27 had left for other reasons, two partly because they felt their opportunities to specialise were restricted. What these figures do not show, moreover, are those within the two-thirds who chose to have their families because of frustrated ambitions or dissatisfaction with other aspects of the job or those who would have returned to work had alternative working arrangements been available. Only one of the leavers interviewed said that she would not be looking for another job in the future. At present there are no opportunities to combine police work and childrearing responsibilities through flexitime, part-time working or job sharing. Of course, the nature of uniform patrol and certain of the specialist departments do not lend themselves readily to these arrangements, but others like Communications, Collators or the Enquiry Office would probably be suitable for adaptation for either women or men who would prefer to work part-time.

Expectations of childrearing responsibilities are therefore fundamental to women's experience of work in the police and the data collected in interviews show evidence of the lowering of aspirations for this reason on the part of some women themselves. In addition, time invested in studying or going away from home on courses required for specialist posts can present problems of role conflict for married women. For those who also have children, it is virtually impossible to leave home even for a short time.

Figure 1: Cause and Effect Spiral. (Jones, 1986, 109)

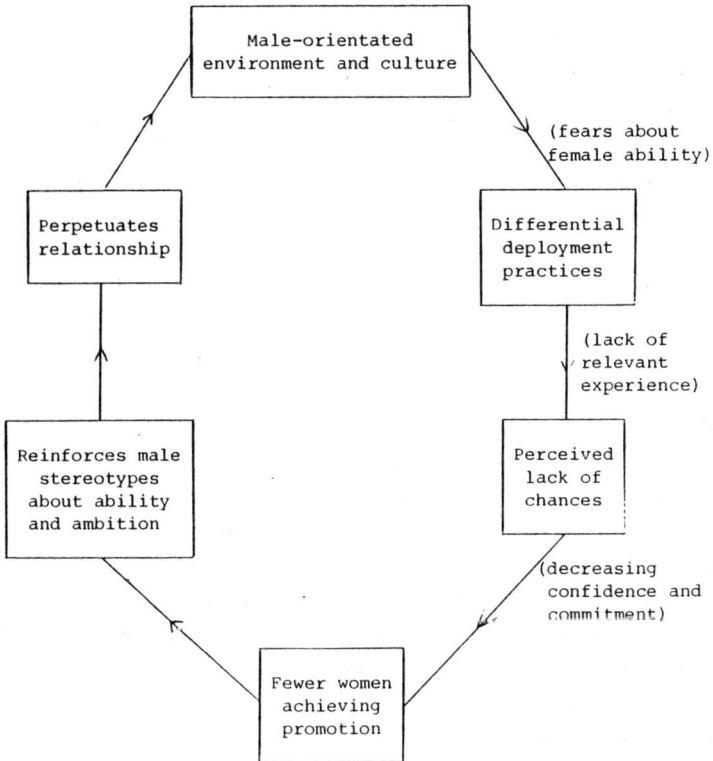

Jones (1986) has described the cycle of underachievement in which many women officers find themselves (Figure 1). Expectations about women's abilities are mediated through the male occupational culture, reinforcing stereotypes. This causes women to be deployed differently from men, with a resulting perception of limited opportunities, contributing to lack of success and, consequently, lack of role models for women. As stated above, data from the present study would suggest a further intervening variable in the cycle: the expectation that women will curtail their careers to have children and a subsequent lowering of their own aspirations. The following comments from two leavers exemplify these positions:

> "I think the opinion that is held is that, 'Oh, she's a woman, she won't be in the police force that long, it's not worth putting all the extra bother to train her - all the money' - because it is expensive."

> "But I had already mapped out my future. I knew roughly when I wanted to start a family, and I knew that there was no point applying for CID or Traffic because I wouldn't be on there very long."

The horizontal occupational segregation of women and men in the police can be seen in Tables 1-3. They show the overrepresentation of women in the research forces on uniform patrol and their underrepresentation in some specialist departments. When all ranks were taken into consideration, whilst 69.4 per cent of all women in Force A were on general patrol, the corresponding figure for men was just 37.0 per cent. The gap was somewhat narrower in the other force where the respective proportions were 57.4 and 48.1 per cent. Similarly, Jones (1986, 57) in 'Medshire', found that although women and men in her sample were represented in roughly equal proportions in uniform patrol and the CID, there was only one female officer on Traffic compared with 6.5 per cent of male officers, and women were overrepresented in clerical and administrative jobs.

The departments where women tended to be employed in greater proportions were, as anticipated, those where their duties were not far removed from their traditional role in policing: for example, the

Youth and Community Service in Force A and Station Duty and Community Constables in Force B. In departments such as the Drugs Squad it was sometimes felt necessary to have some female officers for searching and dealing with women suspects, such that there were so many 'places for women'.

Even where women and men do work together on uniform patrol, there is still some measure of segregation in their deployment. Most female respondents said that generally they did the same work as policemen, but around three-quarters noted that they were also expected to deal with many jobs associated with the former Policewomen's Department. Other aspects mentioned were being excluded from Police Support Units and protected from violent situations, and doing more indoor jobs like station duties and switchboard reliefs. Of the expectations that policewomen will perform 'women's work', a leaver commented:

"... but what I resented was the fact that when I did my training, I did the same training as a policeman and, until I had nearly two years' service in I didn't get any extra training for 'women's work'. But as soon as I came on the station I was expected, if there was a rape reported, to go out and take a brilliant rape statement. Because I'm a woman, I can do it."

Of course, there is some justification for using women officers to interview female victims of sexual assaults, but what is resented is the assumption that the skills necessary in such cases are somehow 'naturally' given to policewomen. Other instances where women officers may be called in preference to a man do not seem justifiable as two officers interviewed pointed out:

"They hear it's a woman and they say, policewoman. If it's a female shoplifter they say policewoman because a lot of the older people working in Communications still haven't changed ... It irritates me sometimes if I'm doing something else and it's something really stupid like a woman's had an indecent telephone call."

"But generally, anything to do with sex, women are called. Even if it's a female missing person, the man who's dealing with it will call you to speak to her before they return her home. So policewomen do get called in for a lot of useless rubbish."

When women do manage to get onto departments where they are underrepresented, as well as having to prove their ability and commitment to gain acceptance, some women felt their minority status added another burden - that of proving the ability of all women in the job:

> "If he (the Inspector) had a bad woman on Traffic, he will go along and say, 'I'm not having any women on Traffic, they're useless'. If they got a good one, then they're prepared to have a second one."

In addition to different deployment experiences, women and men are vertically segregated in the police in that they are not represented in their establishment proportions in the supervisory ranks. Although women now have equality of opportunity to progress through the ranks to Chief Constable, very few even become sergeants. Table 3 shows the establishment figures for the research forces and for England and Wales generally. Although women make up nearly 10 per cent of the total strengths of each force, in the supervisory ranks women represent only 0.4 and 0.8 per cent whilst men in those positions make up 24.5 and 23.4 per cent of the total establishments.

Eight out of 45 respondents who said they might leave the police service gave as their reasons dissatisfaction with their current posts or frustration with the job generally. These sorts of reasons were the most common after family-related reasons and, from the point of view of turnover, are therefore quite significant. Dissatisfaction with prospects may then lead some to look for fulfilment in other areas, either jobs where women predominate or childbearing, reinforcing their gender identity. More respondents said better promotion possibilities were important in encouraging women to stay in the job than other suggested improvements like more pay and flexible hours.

Again, there was a feeling amongst some respondents that they were hindered by expectations of their taking career breaks for childrearing and that men had better opportunities for promotion. A leaver said:

> "I was of the impression that there's not much point in my taking (the exam) because I'm not going to get

promotion ... You stand a lot more chance of getting
promotion if you're a man."

As with specialisation, factors associated with promotion like
geographical mobility are problematic for women who would like to
combine the job with a family. For a few of the leavers it was a case
of their husbands' careers taking precedence over their own in
accordance with the ideology of the male breadwinner. A leaver
commented:

>"Once we got married, I sort of let him take over and I
>took the back seat, sort of thing. I thought it was
>more important for him to be - well, it wouldn't have
>done to have the two of us studying."

Conclusion

There is evidence that women and men are horizontally and vertically
segregated within the police service. However, given the sexual
division of labour reflected in and reinforced by occupational
segregation, perhaps it is not surprising that women working in a
traditionally masculine area do not achieve full equality of
opportunity. Sexual stereotyping does not originate in, nor is it
confined to, the workplace, and the sexual division of labour in the
home influences the way in which women in the job are perceived and
how they perceive themselves. They are thought by some to be more
suitable for 'women's work' for which they have a 'natural' ability,
even though the laws relating to child abuse and procedures to be
followed in cases of alleged rape are quite complex and have to be
learned. Women's opportunities for specialisation and promotion are
hindered by the notion of women as early leavers and therefore less
committed to their jobs than men, a position which might be changed by
the introduction of alternative working arrangements to allow those
with childrearing responsibilities to continue their service.

TABLE 1

Deployment of Constables in Force A in March 1986

	No of women	% of women Con- stables	No of men	% of men Con- stables	Total in Depart- ments	% women in Depart- ments
Uniform Patrol	175	72.9	889	51.8	1064	16.4
Scenes of Crime	-	-	18	1.0	18	-
Crime Prevention	-	-	11	0.6	11	-
Drugs Squad	5	2.1	10	0.6	15	33.3
Vehicle Investigation	-	-	6	0.3	6	-
CID	9	3.7	154	9.0	163	5.5
Criminal Intelligence	-	-	7	0.4	7	-
Station Duty	1	0.4	18	1.0	19	5.3
Communications	7	2.9	52	3.0	59	11.9
Traffic	9	3.7	197	11.5	206	4.4
Collators	1	0.4	9	0.5	10	10.0
Closed Circuit TV	-	-	2	0.1	2	-
Training (Divisions)	-	-	4	0.2	4	-
Gaoler's/Court Duty	1	0.4	24	1.4	25	4.0
Coroner's Office	-	-	9	0.5	9	-
Dogs Section	-	-	27	1.6	27	-
Licencing	1	0.4	3	0.2	4	25.0
Task Force	1	0.4	10	0.6	11	9.0
Youth & Community	8	3.3	17	1.0	25	32.0
Service/Community						
Constables	22	9.2	250	14.6	272	8.0
	240	99.8	1717	99.9	1957	

TABLE 2

Deployment of Constables in Force B in March 1986

	No of women	% of women Con- stables	No of men	% of men Con- stables	Total in Depart- ments	% of women in Depart- ments
Uniform Patrol	62	63.3	495	66.2	557	11.1
Traffic Control Room	3	3.1	22	2.9	25	12.0
Traffic	8	8.2	86	11.5	94	9.3
Ports	1	1.0	15	2.0	16	6.2
Series Crimes Squad	2	2.0	10	1.3	12	16.7
Community Constables	5	5.1	10	1.3	15	33.3
CID (including Aides)	10	10.2	57	7.6	67	14.9
Station Duty	2	2.0	3	0.4	5	40.0
Scenes of Crime	1	1.0	9	1.2	10	10.0
Dogs Section	-	-	12	1.6	12	-
Marine Section	-	-	6	0.8	6	-
Fraud Section	-	-	2	0.3	2	-
Special Branch	-	-	3	0.4	3	-
Drugs & Vice Squads	4	4.1	16	2.1	20	20
Training	-	-	2	0.3	2	-
	98	100	748	99.9		

TABLE 3

Establishments of the Research Forces and Total Establishment in
England and Wales (including the Metropolitan Police) at 31st
December, 1985

	Men	Women	Men	Women	Men	Women	Ratio
Chief Constable (CC)	1	-	1	-	48	-	
Deputy CC	1	-	1	-	57	-	
Assistant CC	3	-	1	-	133	2	1:66
Chief Superintendent	13	-	6	-	633	9	1:70
Superintendent	36	1	15	2	1,514	27	1:56
Chief Inspector	53	0	21	1	2,304	49	1:47
Inspector	134	5	66	0	6,537	132	1:49
Sergeant	442	6	170	7	18,856	626	1:30
Constables	1,838	259	808	103	79,317	10,458	1:7.6
	2,521	271	1,089	113	109,399	11,303	1:9.7
		9.7%		9.4%		9.4%	

References

Alexander S. (1976) Women's Work in Nineteenth Century London: A
        study of the Years 1820-1850, in A. Oakley and J. Mitchell
        (Eds) The Rights and Wrongs of Women, Penguin, Harmondsworth.

Davin A. (1978) Imperialism and Motherhood, History Workshop Journal,
        Issue 5.

Hilton J. (1975) Women in the Police Service, Police Journal,
        Vol XLIX, 2, pp 93-103.

Homans H. (1987) Man-made Myths: The Reality of Being a Woman
        Scientist in the NHS, in A. Spencer and D. Podmore (Eds) In a
        Man's World: Essays on Women in Male-Dominated Professions,
        Tavistock, London.

Jones S. (1986) Policewomen and Equality: Formal Policy v Informal
        Practice? Macmillan, London.

Mort F. (1986) Purity, feminism and the state: sexuality and moral
        politics, 1880-1914, in M. Langan and B. Schwarz (Eds) Crises
        in the British State 1880-1930. Hutchinson, London.

Oakley A. (1981) Subject Women, Fontana, London.

Punch M. (1979) The police as a secret social service, in S. Holdaway
        (Ed) The British Police. Edward Arnold, London.

Sherman L.J. (1973) A psychological view of women in policing,
        Journal of Police Science and Administration, Vol 1, No 4.

Smith D. and Gray J. (1983) Police and the People in London: The
        Police in Action, Vols 1-4, Policy Studies Institute.

CHIEF CONSTABLES: A CHANGING ELITE

D Wall

Research Officer

Centre for Criminology and Criminal Justice

University of Hull

Introduction

The office of chief constable is currently defined by the Police Act
1964 which is very vague in its outline of the duties of the chief
constable and the boundaries of his accountability. The chief
constable, unlike other local officials, has a great deal of autonomy
in his decision making which is exercised without much formal
accountability. In the absence of a formal structure of accountability
authors such as Jefferson and Grimshaw (1984) have emphasised the
importance of informal networks of accountability. But if informal
networks are important in the absence of formal structures then who
chief constables are may be as important as what they are.

It soon becomes apparent when reading through the literature on
policing that whilst much has been written on the lives, careers and
social origins of police officers none of this applies to chief
constables. As Reiner notes:

"Whilst we have some knowledge of the social origins and

previous careers of recruits we do not have this
information for senior officers." (Reiner 1982, 173)

This paper will draw upon on-going research (Wall, forthcoming)[1] to
examine, historically, the policies which governed the choice of chief
constable and the origins of the people who were appointed to it.

The Development of the Office of Chief Constable

Before the Local Government Act 1973 caused the police area boundaries
to be redrawn the provincial police of England and Wales was composed
of county and borough forces each of which had a different statutory
background.

The Municipal Corporations Acts of 1835 and 1882 provided for the
installation of borough forces and the County Police Act 1839 and
Local Government Act 1888 for the county forces. Only in the county
forces was there any provision for the appointment, by the police
authority with the approval of the Home Secretary, of a chief officer:
known as chief constable. The Municipal Corporations Acts vested in
the borough police authority (the watch committee) the same powers
that were granted to the county chief constable. The Municipal
Corporations Act made no mention of a chief officer of police and the
post was not given statutory force until 1919. The post of borough
chief constable 'emerged' out of the impracticalities of having a
watch committee, which had neither the skills nor the time to, take
the responsibility for policing the borough.

The Selection and Appointment of Chief Constables before 1919

The formal procedure of selecting a chief constable has not changed
much over the years. The police authority still advertises the
vacancy, draws up a shortlist, interviews, ballots its members for
their choice of candidate and then seeks the Home Secretary's approval
for the appointment. The informal aspects of the selection process
have, however, changed. The police authority can no longer choose

- 85 -

whoever it pleases to fill the post. All candidates now have to be approved in advance by the Home Office which takes into consideration the candidates performance in both their force and on the senior command course at the Police Staff College.

Before the Desborough Committee recommended in 1919 that only persons with police experience be appointed as chief constables (Home Office 1919), the only guidelines regarding the appointment of chief constables came from rules made by the Home Secretary under the County Police Act 1839. The Home Secretary's rules stated that chief constables:

> "... must be certified by a medical practitioner to be in good health and of sound constitution, and fitted to perform the duties of the office." [and] "... must be recommended to the Secretary of State by the Police Committee, in whom the appointment is vested, as a person of general good character and conduct." (Home Secretary's Rules, 1857)

These vague rules did not apply to the appointment of borough chief officers.

County Chief Constables

In the absence of any direction on the qualities a chief constable must possess the police authorities were given a free hand to appoint whoever they wanted and the persons they tended to appoint were ex-army officers:

> "... who at any rate were men of education, with a knowledge of the world, accustomed to discipline and to the management of men and whose personal qualities were generally known to those making the appointments." (Nott-Bower, 1926, 324)

The 23 chief constables who were appointed under the non-compulsory County Police Act 1839 all had officer experience and tended to come from landed families. About one third of that number also had some experience of police work from either the Metropolitan Police, the Royal Irish Constabulary (R.I.C) or the borough forces. These first chief constables were appointed in their early to mid-forties after an army career of about 21 years and stayed in office for 20 to 30 years; leaving office in their early 70s. Over a third died whilst they were 'still in harness'. (Wall, forthcoming).

When the County and Borough Police Act 1856 made the installation of police forces compulsory the chief constables who were chosen to command the 24 new forces were men with the same backgrounds as those appointed before the Act but, overall, they had less experience of policing (Steedman 1984). Their average age at appointment was also the same as those appointed before 1856 but they stayed in office much longer leaving office whilst in their late 70s or early eighties (Wall, forthcoming). These observations tally with those of Steedman (1984) who found that the 24 chief constables appointed immediately after the Act of 1856 stayed in office for an average of 24 years each. Six actually stayed in office for over 30 years and two for over 40 years.

The county police authorities did not need to consider what qualities they would require in their chief constable until the latter part of the 19th century by which time the pattern was set. All of the replacement chief constables appointed during the 1890s, with the exception of the chief constable of Rutland whose command was less than 10 men, were from the same county backgrounds as their predecessors. It is interesting to note that half of the chief constables appointed between 1905 and 1915 died in office, compared with only 15% of their predecessors (Wall, forthcoming).

An examination of the inclusion of county chief constables in contemporary directories of elites, such as Who's Who and Kelly's Handbook of Official and Titled Classes, revealed that over three-quarters of those in office in 1905 had an entry in one or the other. The inclusion of county chief constables in such directories was by virtue of their background rather than their occupation. The county chief constableship became a popular occupation for the younger sons of the landed gentry in the same way that the army and cloth had done:

> "Becoming head of a county force might enable a man to consolidate and extend an existing social position and

wed himself to the upper reaches of the county
hierarchy." (Steedman, 1984 47)

Particularly after the Crimean war when the chances of promotion in
the army were reduced, many frustrated young officers, like Nott-Bower
(1926), opted for a police career rather than wait many years for
promotion.

The social backgrounds of the first county chief constables and their
sucessors were similar to those of the members of the quarter
sessions. In 1888, after the Local Government Act of that year the
quarter sessions were replaced by the half elected SJC. This change
threatened to open membership of the county police authority to other
social groups if they were elected. But, recent unpublished research
(Buckle, forthcoming) [2] has shown that in reality there was little
change as most of the first county councillors were, if not themselves
justices, of the same landed gentry stock as the justices.

By appointing a chief constable with a similar world outlook to
themselves the county police authority could be fairly certain that he
would not only have an understanding of their position in the local
social hierarchy but would also share the same social and governmental
assumptions (Steedman, 1984). Once a chief constable was appointed he
exercised a great deal of autonomy in his control over policing in the
county and could not be removed from office arbitrarily. The police
authority could only exercise informal means to influence policing;
the most potent of which was controlling the purse strings of the
county force.

The county chief constables were from very different backgrounds to
those under their command. In the 19th century a policeman's pay was
based upon the wages of an agricultural labourer and many of the first
policemen were chosen from that occupation (Phillips, 1977; Emsley,
1983; Steedman, 1984). The tradition of paying low wages was set by
Peel in order to deter gentlemen from joining the police (Gash, 1961).
Peel's intention was to prevent the police from becoming as class
ridden as the army and in the Metropolitan police the commissioners

were, until recently, justices and not policemen. However Peel's idea backfired in the provinces as a commissioned/non-commisioned divide between the lower and very senior ranks developed.

Borough Chief Constables

The origins of the first borough chief officers were very different to those of the county chief constables. The non-statutory nature of the office meant that the borough chief officer, where one was appointed, was an employee of the watch committee who could be hired and fired at will. It would seem that this was the fate of many of the first chief officers. As many as 40% of the borough chief officers appointed between 1836 and 1845 were dismissed from office; although only about 5% of those appointed between 1846 and 1855 shared the same fate (Wall, forthcoming).

The turnover of borough chief officers due to transfer to another force was also high. About one third of the borough chief officers appointed between 1846 and 1855 left to take command of another borough force. In each case the transfer was to a larger sized command (Wall, forthcoming).

As the size of borough forces grew with enforced amalgamations and an overall increase in the establishment of the police, the posts of chief officer in the remaining forces became more firmly established. By the turn of the century most borough chief officers were referred to as chief constable even though the smallest borough command of between 10 and 15 man was over 100 times smaller than the largest. Rather ironically it was the largest borough force, Liverpool, which insisted on retaining the title of head constable for its chief officer, until the Police Act 1919 changed it, long after others had subsumed to using chief constable.

The men who became the early borough chief officers were invariably policemen; many were officers from the Metropolitan police who were drafted in to help install a police force (Hart 1955). A typical

borough chief constable before the first world war would have joined a
police force whilst in his early twenties and served for about ten
years, rising to inspector, before being appointed to a small force in
his early thirties. After a few years experience in a small force it
was common for them to move to a larger force in their mid to late
thirties. Most served for about fifteen years before retiring in their
early fifties. Appointments to the medium sized forces tended to be of
older men with many years service or of a younger person with
experience of command in a number of forces. The very large boroughs
competed for the same candidates as did the counties although the
careers of the men chosen were in the professions rather than the
military (Wall, forthcoming).

The social backgrounds of borough chief constables in the 19th century
were very different to those of the county chief constables described
earlier. They were from the working, and lower middle, classes
although the chiefs of the larger borough forces shared many social
characteristics with the county chief constables. An idea of how
different their backgrounds were in comparison to the county chief
constables can be illustrated by comparing entries in elite
directories. Only about 5% of the 127 borough chief constables in
office in 1905, typically those in command of the very large borough
forces, had an entry in either Who's Who or Kelly's Handbook.

The demands made by the watch committee of their chief constable were
different to those made by the county police authority of their chief
constable. The county police authority wanted a person with a similar
outlook to themselves, possibly with social or familial links as well,
who they could trust to police the county according to its version of
the world. The watch committee, in comparison, merely wanted an
employee who could be trusted to carry out orders. Thus the borough
chief constableship became a reward for dutiful service rather than a
recognition of competance as a policeman.

Over the years there have been many allegations that freemasonry
played an important part in promotions within the police. Certainly
many borough chief constables were, and openly admitted to being,

freemasons during the last century. In 1885 as many as three quarters of borough chief constables were freemasons although by the turn of the century that figure had reduced to only about a third. This apparent recuction could however reflect a growing reluctance on the part of chief constables to reveal their membership in the face of allegations of masonic interference in promotions. Few of the allegations against freemasonry were in fact substantiated in any way and whether or not freemasonry played a significant role in appointments is debateable. There existed many other organisations and bodies in which policemen were also involved and which also must be taken into consideration. What is certain is that there was a general disquiet over the grounds on which appointments to chief constable were made in both the counties and boroughs. In his evidence to the Desborough Committee in 1919 one of Her Majesty's Inspectors of Constabulary said that he thought that chief constables were appointed:

> "not on their merits as policemen, especially in the smaller boroughs." (Home office, 1920, 88)

The Selection of Chief Constables after 1919

A number of issues came to a head at the end of the first World War and culminated in the police strikes of 1918 and 1919. One of the issues which contributed to the crisis was the idiosyncratic way in which chief constables were selected, particularly as policemen in the lower ranks could not reasonably expect to gain promotion beyond the rank of superintendent. The Desborough Committee inquired into the appointment of chief constables and was presented with arguments from those who favoured the retention of the present system and those who wanted a fully professional police service with all senior officers having served in the police throughout their careers. The committee's recommendations were a compromise between the two view points:

> "We recommend that no person without previous police experience should be appointed as chief constable in any force unless he possesses some exceptional qualification or experience which specially fits him for the post, or there is no other candidate from the police service who is considered sufficiently well qualified." (Home Office, 1919 para 139)

This recommendation became incorporated into the rules that the Police Act 1919 empowered the Home Secretary to make in order to govern the pay, conditions of service and appointments of the police. It became known as Regulation 9 and it was the first time that an attempt had been made to prescribe the qualities a police authority should look for in a chief constable.

For a variety of reasons the effect of Regulation 9 was mixed. On the one hand an examination of the previous occupations of chief constables prior to their first command reveals that the percentage of county chief constables from police occupations increased after the introduction of Regulation 9. On the other hand the increase in appointments from police occupations was a continuation of a trend towards the selection of men from police occupations that had started in the mid-19th century.

Whilst there was a move on the part of police authorities towards selecting chief constables from the police the extent to which this change was in any way contributable to Regulation 9 can be questioned. The wording of Regulation 9 was loose enough to allow police authorities, particularly in the counties, to 'creatively' interpret the rule and thus minimalise its effect. They either appointed men with colonial police or R.I.C backgrounds or appointed ex-army men directly as assistant chief constables, a post that was traditionally 'in the gift' of the chief constable and not covered by Regulation 9; hence the apparent modification of selection practices. Once a person had served as an assistant chief constable then he could claim that experience in order to qualify for chief constable whenever a vacancy arose.

The apparent change in selection practices, described above, was an attempt by the county police authorities to accommodate the changes that were being pressed upon them. The police authorities saw Regulation 9 as an attempt to usurp their powers and influence over policing and were naturally hostile towards it.

The extent to which police authorities evaded Regulation 9 can be illustrated when the occupational origins of chief constables serving in 1908 are compared with those serving in 1939.

In his evidence to the 1908 Select Committee on the Police Weekly rest day, John Kempster, then editor of the Police Review informed the committee that only 3 of the 44 English county chief constables had risen through the ranks. Of that number 33 were ex-army officers and the rest were a combination of colonial policemen and gentry all with army experience. In Wales, because of the need for a Welsh speaking chief chief constable, half of the chiefs had served as policemen; the rest were ex-army officers. In contrast to the origins of the county chief constables only 15 of the 123 borough chief constables had not risen through the ranks of a British police force.

Thirty one years later, just before the outbreak of the second world war, only four of the 42 English chief constables, one more than in 1908, had been in the police service throughout their careers. Similarly only six of the 117 borough chief constables had not risen through the ranks (Home Office, 1967, 8; Wall, forthcoming).

The Propagation of Home Grown Chief Constables

During the 1920s the idea of the home grown chief officer gained currency, not least because of the new professional ethos which crept into policing as a result of the Desborough recommendations on higher pay, better conditions and centralised training. The issue of who should command a police force was the subject of much discussion amongst the various bodies concerned and opinions on the matter were polarised between the professionalists and traditionalists. The former favoured a professionally integrated police in which all senior officers would have served in the lower ranks whereas the latter, supported by The Royal Commission on Police Procedures and Powers (1929), wanted the best men for the job regardless of their training or previous occupation. However, Picton-Davies (1973) argues that the Royal Commission was merely reflecting public opinion after the

Savidge case in which senior officers were blamed for the misconduct of their men. The Royal Comission's view-point also conflicted with current opinion in senior police and Home Office circles. In his report on the inspection of constabulary for 1929 Mr de Courcy-Parry commented that:

> "there is probably no other profession in the country where a man of no experience can be placed in such a responsible position." (De Courcy-Parry, 1929)

The tide of opinion was flowing towards the professionalisation of the upper ranks but a problem existed in so far as the type of person who police authorities normally associated with a command position was not to be found in the ranks of the police. The police were not attracting recruits with the relevant educational qualities to suit them for command. Whereas the general provision of secondary education throughout England and Wales had been increased by five times, the police were recruiting people with the same educational attainment as in the 19th century. Therefore a system was needed to bring out and train men who had command capabilities. A variety of schemes were put forward to facilitate the training of senior officer from within the police. The Home Office's idea for a National Police College to train serving policemen was proposed and rejected on financial grounds, as was an idea for the introduction of a sponsored cadet scheme similar to that proposed by Nott-Bower (1926). The scheme that was accepted was Trenchard's proposal for a Metropolitan Police College.

Based on his experience in commanding the R.A.F. Trenchard wanted to create an officer class in order to solve the problem of finding men for the senior ranks from within the Metropolitan Police. Recruits to the college would be inducted through a course of tuition at a newly formed Police College at Hendon. On successful completion of the course they would gain automatic promotion to inspector. To allow the Hendon men to rise quickly through the ranks the promotion of all Metropolitan police officers appointed after 1933 was frozen. The scheme aroused great hostility from within the lower ranks of the Metropolitan police.

The college opened in 1934 and before closing at the outbreak of war 188 graduates passed through its doors; 132 had entered from the Metropolitan police and 56 as direct entrants through either open selection or open examination. The recruits to the college were what Trenchard referred to as 'officer material' and were drawn primarily from the middle classes (Wall, forthcoming). The legacy of Hendon was to be felt most of all in the years after the war.

After the outbreak of war no chief constables were appointed to their first appointment without having served in the ranks. This was due to a combination of policy, the wartime regulations which increased the Home Secretary's powers over the police and police authorities, and also the fact that many of the army officer candidates for chief constableships had rejoined their regiments. In 1946, after the wartime regulations ended, the Post-War Committee on the Reconstruction of the Police Service gave force to the policy that all future chief constables were to have served throughout their careers as police officers.

At a time when police authorities, particularly in the counties, were resistant to the changes being forced upon them the presence of the Hendon graduates in the pool of candidates for senior appointments enabled them to appoint the type of people they wanted and also not fall foul of the Home Secretary's rules.

The Hendon men came to dominate the most senior ranks in the police service until the early 1970s. In 1965 the Commissioner, deputy commissioner and four assistant commissioners in the Metropolitan Police, 19 county chief constables, six borough chief constables, the Chief Inspector of Constabulary and three of his collegues were all trained at Hendon (From figures complied by Webb quoted by Picton-Davies 1973).

The Metropolitan Police College was not reopened after the war. Instead a National Police College was formed to train serving officers in the intermediate ranks in command. In 1960 that college was moved from Ryton-on-Dunsmore to its present location at Bramshill House. A series of scandals in the 1950s which involved chief constables led to the Royal Commission on the Police in 1960 considering the issue of senior command. When looking at chief constables and their training the Commission identified the need to attract more educated recruits into the police to improve the quality of the police and more senior positions. But it found:

> "...no recent instance of a university graduate entering the service;" (Royal Commission on the Police, 1962 Para. 308)

and that less than a third of all recruits had GCE passes.

In 1961 a white paper entitled Police Training in England and Wales followed the Commission's initial findings on the quality of police recruits. The paper proposed: firstly a special course for constables with the most outstanding marks giving automatic promotion to sergeant; secondly, a proportion of the places on the existing course which prepares sergeants for promotion to inspector was also to be open to sergeants who qualified by examination. At the time all entry to the course was by recommendation of the chief constable. Thirdly, a senior staff course, of a primarily professional character, was to be introduced to equip officers at the rank of inspector and above for the highest posts in the service. The white paper intended these courses to:

> "improve the ability of the Police Service to attract and train its own leaders, and enable the Police College to make an even greater contribution than at present to the efficiency of the service." (Police Training in England and Wales, 1961)

These proposals provided a foundation for the four main courses that are run at the Police Staff College, as it is now called. Each course prepares officers for promotion to the next rank.

Whilst the proposals for training catered for serving officers, the need was identified to attract more highly qualified recruits into the police and a graduate entry scheme was also introduced, although the numbers who enter by it are small. This scheme is complemented by the Bramshill scholarship, introduced in 1964, to offer police officers who had slipped through the educational net an opportunity to take up higher education.

The Police Staff College has had a marked effect on the senior ranks. All candidates for chief constableships today are graduates of the senior command course and a growing number of those appointed are ex-special course. By the 1990s it is very probable that the majority of new chief constables will be graduates of the special course and that the average age at their first command will fall. The average age on appointment as chief constable in the latter part of the 19th century rose from about 40 (which represented the age at which an army officer can retire on pension after 21 years service - see earlier), to between 55 and 60 in the early 1980s after 30 to 35 years police service. The special course graduates tend to rise through the ranks to chief contable after 20 to 25 years service and be appointed to their first command in their mid-to late 40s, or even younger (Wall, forthcoming).

The Social Origins of Chief Constables

The social origins of today's chief constables (sampled between 1975 and 1985) were found to be very different to those of their predecessors. Whereas all county chief constables at the turn of the century, with the exception of very small forces such as Rutland, were either from the upper middle and titled classes, the majority of chief constables today come from middle and lower middle class backgrounds. They were educated at grammar and state schools in contrast to their predecessors who until the second world war were mostly educated at the Clarendon list public schools.

Just over two thirds of the modern chief constables sampled attended a further education institution on either a full or part time basis. Half went to a university (typically redbrick) and the rest to a technical college. Two thirds had some sort of higher academic qualification: one third had a certificate or diploma and the other third a degree. The majority of those academic qualifications were also professionally oriented with the diplomas and certificates tending to be in management and the degrees being in law (Wall, forthcoming).

One sign of the growing status of the office of chief constable over the years has been the inclusion of most of its incumbents in Who's Who. Today just over half of serving chief constables have an entry in Who's Who. They are there because of what they are whereas their predecessors were included in an directory of elites because of who they were. It will be remembered that over three-quarters of the county chief constables in office in 1905 had an entry in either Who's who or Kelly's Handbook of the Official and Titled Classes.

Conclusion

This paper has illustrated the extent to which the office of chief constable today is very different to its county and borough predecessors.

Where chief constables were once part of the local power elite; in the counties the gentry and in the boroughs, to a lesser extent, the local municipal elite, they are now an elite group in their own right. A professional elite bounded by specialist training, a professional association, a professional ethos and a unique autonomy amongst local government public service officials.

Footnotes

1.   This paper is based upon ongoing research into the selection and origins of the 1735 appointments to chief constable who are known to have held office in England and Wales between 1835 and 1985. It will be published as an MPhil dissertation later this year by the Department of Social Policy and Social Work at the University of York. All references to Wall, forthcoming refer to this work.   The data on which the research is based was

compiled from publically available sources such as Who's Who,
Kelly's Handbook the Police Review and the autobiographies of
ex-chief constables. The scale of the lack of information was
realised at the outset of the research when it was found that
there did not exist a list of the names of all of the chief
constables in England and Wales.

2.   Buckle, H L, 'Power and Authority in the East Riding of
      Yorkshire from 1888 to 1940', MPhil dissertation to be
      submitted to Hull College of Higher Education.

References

Critchley, T A, (1966). A History of Police in England and Wales
        900-1966. London: Constable.

Davies, Graham P, (1973). The Police Services of England and Wales
        Between 1918 and 1964. PhD Thesis LSE, 1973.

De Courcy-Parry, (1929). Report of His Majesty's Inspector of
        Constabulary. London: HMSO.

Emsley, C, (1983). Policing and Its Context 1750-1870.   London:
        Macmillan.

Gash, N, (1961). Mr Secretary Peel. London: Longman.

Hart, J, (1955). 'The Reform of the Borough Police, 1835-1856' in
        English Historical Review, Vol 70, p 411.

Home Office, (1919). Committee on the Police Service of England,
        Wales and Scotland, Part I, Cmd 513. London: HMSO.

Home Office, (1920). Committee on the Police Service of England,
        Wales and Scotland, Part II, (The Desborough Report).
        London: HMSO.

Home Office, (1967). The Recruitment of People with Higher
        Educational Qualifications into the Police Service:
        Report of a Working Party. London: HMSO.

Jefferson, T and Grimshaw, R, (1984). Controlling the Contable:
        Police Accountability in England and Wales. London: Miller/
        The Cobden Trust.

Nott-Bower, S R W, (1926). 52 Years a Policeman. London: Arnold.

Phillips, D, (1977). Crime and Authority in Victorian England.
        London: Croom Helm.

Police Training in England and Wales, (1961). Cmd 1450. London:
        HMSO.

Reiner, R, (1982). 'Who Are the Police?' Political Quarterley 53/2.

Royal Commission on the Police. Final Report, Cmd 1728. London:
        HMSO.

Royal Commission on Police Powers and Procedures. Report 16/3/1929.
        London: HMSO.

Steedman, C, (1984). Policing The Victorian Community. London:
        Routledge.